THE UNEXPECTED JOURNEY

ME AND AUTISM

Angeline Shanta

INDIA · SINGAPORE · MALAYSIA

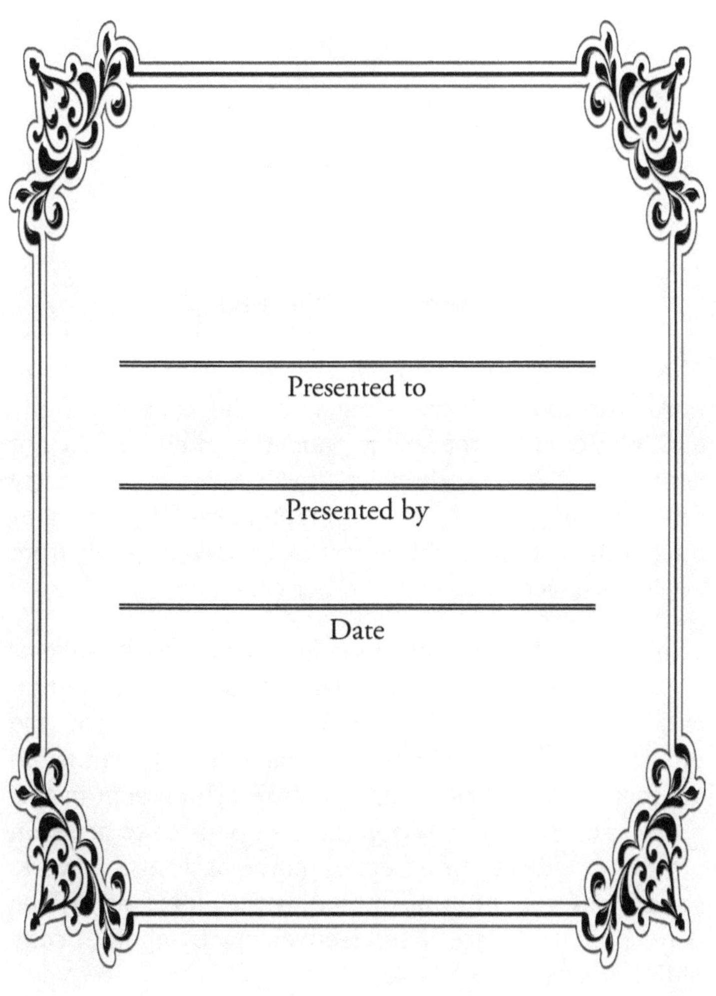

Presented to

Presented by

Date

ISBN
Paperback 979-8-89744-997-2
Hardcase 979-8-89961-306-7

Dedication

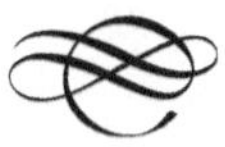

To my heavenly parents, **Bhaskaran Pillay** & **Vimala Nair**, whose love and blessings continue to guide me.

To my dear siblings, **Chandrika** & **Shivan Pillay**, for their support and love.

A heartfelt thank you to my cousins, relatives, teachers therapists, coaches, and friends who have been there for me throughout this journey.

A special thank you to all the parents I have met along the way, your stories, strength, and kindness have meant so much to me.

To my dearest son, thank you for being the wonderful person you are. I am so proud of all your progress and accomplishments. I will always love you.

Thank you.

Contents

Dear God,

If I can make one wish, I will wish for my son to be surrounded with kind, loving, helpful people. People who love him as he is – special in his own way.

He may be difficult to be understood, maybe that's why his way of showing love and express feelings seems unique.

He may find it difficult to speak, maybe that's why he expresses different emotions.

He may find it difficult accepting and understanding instructions maybe that's why he does things differently.

Judging him will never be fair to him because God has made him Special in his own way.

God, when my time on earth is over, kindly hold his hands and guide him to the right path with good Samaritans around him.

Graciously accept my humble wish God.

With love,

– Angeline Shanta

Preface

When I think back to the last 18 years, I see a journey full of lessons, challenges, and moments of hope. Supporting my son through his progress has taught me so much. Over the years, I attended many trainings, gained new knowledge, and faced challenges that pushed me to grow. Along the way, I met kind and supportive people who motivated me and gave me the strength to keep going.

The idea of writing this book has been in my mind for a long time. After going through this journey with my son, I feel it is time to share what I've learned. If I could look back 18 years ago and compare it to where we are now, I would see how much I have grown and how far we've come. I want to share that journey with you.

This book is my way of reaching out to parents and families who are facing challenges like mine. I want to inspire you through my experiences and give you a guide that you can turn to when you need support or direction.

I hope that reading about my journey will help you find strength in your own. I hope it reminds you that even though the path may feel hard at times, you are not alone. Through this book, my wish is to share what I've learned and inspire you to keep moving forward.

Chapter 1

My Life Before and After My Son's Diagnosis

I'm a Mother

I'm a mother. It's the most important thing in my life. Being a mother is about more than just having a baby. It's about loving, caring, and always being there. It's about making tough choices and trying to do what's best for your child.

When I became a mother, my life changed in many ways. I learned to put my child first. Every smile from my child made all the sleepless nights and worries worth it. I found strength I didn't know I had because I wanted to give my child the best life. There are moments of joy and moments of struggle. Sometimes you feel like you're doing everything wrong, but then you see your child happy and know that every hard moment was worth it. It's a journey filled with love, patience, and learning. The joy of seeing my child's first steps, hearing their first words, and watching them grow filled my heart with so much pride and happiness.

Each child is unique. Being a mother to my child meant understanding and accepting that uniqueness. For me, it meant learning how to raise a child with Autism Spectrum Disorder. It meant finding new ways to communicate, connect, and support my child.

I'm a mother, and every day, I am thankful for my child and the journey we share.

Okay, I'll start. I got married in 1999. In 2000, I found out I was pregnant for the first time. I was so happy. The thought of becoming a mother filled me with joy. I imagined holding my baby, watching them grow, and sharing my love with them.

But at three months, I had a miscarriage. Losing the baby was very hard. It felt like my world had shattered. I had so many hopes and dreams, and suddenly, they were gone.

In 2002, I got pregnant again. This time, I was hopeful but also very careful. I wanted everything to be okay. But at seven months, I gave birth to a stillborn child. Holding my baby, who couldn't take a breath, was the hardest thing I've ever done. My heart was broken, and I felt so lost. After this, I sort of gave up. I told myself that if it was meant to be, I would get pregnant again. But deep down, I was very scared.

Then, in 2007, I found out I was pregnant again. The fear and hope were both there. Every doctor's visit was filled with anxiety, but I tried to stay positive. This time, things were different. Jeremy was born. When I held him for the first time, it was like all the pain of the past went away. He was perfect, and he was my son.

Jeremy was born a healthy child. My delivery was a caesarean because he did not complete nine months. The umbilical cord was tangled around his neck, so the doctor decided to proceed with the caesarean. Other than that, he was a healthy baby.

Four days after he was born, he developed jaundice. He spent one whole day in the incubator, under the light. It was a worrying time, but the doctors assured me it was common. The next day, he was discharged and came home with us. That was the only major incident. After that, his development was normal.

From newborn to infant, Jeremy's growth followed the usual stages. He first turned onto his belly, then started crawling using his hands. After that, he was crawling all over the place. He stood up by holding onto a chair and gradually gained strength and balance.

His walking was a bit delayed. Jeremy only started walking on his own confidently at one year and seven months. I remember feeling a mix of worry and hope during those months.

Once he reached the toddler's age, one to three, Jeremy was growing as expected. There is a chart that shows what a toddler should be doing at each age, like walking, playing, and talking. Jeremy followed this chart in most areas. He was active, curious, and learning new things every day.

According to the chart, toddlers should start to speak more words as they grow. By age one, they might say a few words like "mama" or "dada." By age two, they should know around 50 words and start putting them together into short phrases. By age three, they should be able to speak in simple sentences.

Jeremy was different in this area. He wasn't saying as many words as the chart said he should. While other children his age were starting to talk more, Jeremy was still using only a few words. This worried me a bit, but I tried not to overthink it.

I remembered that some family members had similar experiences. Some kids in my family didn't start talking much until after they turned three, but then they began talking a lot. So, I thought maybe Jeremy was just taking his time. I hoped that, like my relatives, he would start talking more when he was ready.

Even though his speech was delayed, I believed he would catch up in his own time. I didn't think it should be associated with autism. I watched and waited, hoping his words would come soon.

Jeremy is a cheerful child. He is hyperactive but definitely a happy child. He reacted to TV children's programs with great excitement. I bought children's educational CDs for him and played them. One time, the program asked the child watching to say, "Blast off," while raising their hands up. Jeremy followed along perfectly. The interaction was there, he was engaging and responding. He was learning and growing just like other kids his age.

Discovering Autism

Personally, at that time, I had heard about ASD (Autism Spectrum Disorder), but I didn't really know the details. I assumed all was fine. When Jeremy was three years old, I visited a pediatrician because Jeremy's nose was bleeding. I wanted to check and see what was going on.

When we entered the clinic, the doctor, instead of checking Jeremy's nose right away, interacted with him. He asked us if we had noticed anything different about Jeremy. We said no, thinking Jeremy was just like any other child. Then the doctor said Jeremy was showing signs of autism. We were shocked.

The doctor said the nose bleeding wasn't the main issue. He pointed out two things: when we called Jeremy's name, he didn't respond immediately, and he had poor eye contact. These are two main characteristics of children with autism. The doctor tested this in front of us. He called Jeremy's name several times before Jeremy reacted. When the doctor tried to look into Jeremy's eyes, Jeremy looked away and didn't make eye contact. This was the first time we heard that Jeremy might have autism.

The pediatrician told us it might be shocking to hear this for the first time. He suggested we print out the symptoms from a website and check all the signs because, as he said, parents know their children better than a doctor seeing them for the first time. He also advised us to enroll Jeremy in an Early Intervention Program (EIP). The sooner we started therapy, the better the progress could be. Jeremy was only three years old at the time.

We got the medication for Jeremy's nose bleeding and went back home, feeling brokenhearted. We kept asking ourselves,

"Why us? Why Jeremy?" He was such a cute little boy, and now we were facing this new challenge. We were all very sad.

I was crying non-stop. I couldn't accept it. I was so shocked to know that Jeremy has autism. We don't have any family history of autism. Normally, when you go for an assessment to check if a child has autism, the first question they ask is if there is any family history. My answer was no.

The second question was if there were any complications during the pregnancy. For me, I did not complete the pregnancy, and Jeremy was born via cesarean. Then, they follow a checklist to see if the child fits the criteria for ASD (Autism Spectrum Disorder) or ADHD (Attention Deficit Hyperactivity Disorder). But as soon as they see that the child does not have eye contact or doesn't respond when called, they suspect autism.

When I did the checklist, most of the answers pointed to ADHD symptoms. But on the ASD list, the lack of eye contact and not responding when called were the obvious signs. When I went to hospitals for further assessment, the doctors said, "Madam, these two are the major symptoms of an autistic child."

Even though Jeremy showed more ADHD symptoms, the doctors explained that because of these two major symptoms, no eye contact and not responding when called, they would categorize him under autism. From there, they advised on the next steps to take, including proper therapy, the right school, and treatment for Jeremy.

We were thinking, what are we going to do, and how are we going to do it? We informed our family members. Everyone was shocked and sad. I started searching on Google for special needs schools that specifically take children with autism. Just as the pediatrician suggested, I brought Jeremy to a psychologist for an assessment to confirm the diagnosis.

The psychologist confirmed that Jeremy has autism and also has some ASD characteristics. This news was hard to accept, but we needed to move forward and find the best support for Jeremy. We began searching for schools and therapies that could help him. Every time you bring a child with autism to a new school or therapy, they do an assessment. It's like an interview to see what the child knows and to identify the symptoms. Each place we visited said Jeremy had ASD, but my heart told me to go for a second opinion.

To those reading this book, if you have just found out that your child has autism, it's okay to seek a second opinion. It's important to understand the professional's point of view and get their advice and guidance. So, I went for a second opinion, and they also confirmed that Jeremy has autism.

This confirmation was difficult, but it helped us to know for sure. It gave us a clearer path forward to get Jeremy the help and support he needed. We started looking into the best therapies and schools to support his development.

To get further advice, I decided to go to KK Women's and Children's Hospital in Singapore, which specializes in children's special needs. The doctors there were very well-qualified, and I received a lot of useful advice and guidelines. In Singapore, if a child is diagnosed with autism, they offer a training program for parents. They train, advise, and guide parents on how to handle a child with autism. This was something we didn't have back home in Malaysia.

Since we didn't have such programs in Malaysia, we had to do our own research. We sought advice from the private sector, therapists, and special needs schools. We educated ourselves about autism and how to support children with it.

Moving Forward

From here on, this book will delve into the steps, guidelines, and advice I wish I had known from the start. If I had known what I know now from the beginning, things might have been different from day one. I want parents of children with autism to have this information early on to make their children's lives better.

We will explore what to do and what not to do, how to seek the right help, and how to support your child effectively. This book will cover various aspects of raising a child with autism, providing practical tips and personal insights. I hope that this guide will help other parents find their journey with more ease and confidence.

There isn't one method that works for every child with autism because every child is different. What helps one child might not work for another, and that's completely fine. Each day is a chance to learn and try new things. Every suggestion you hear or idea you try will teach you something. If something doesn't work, don't feel upset, it just means it wasn't the right fit for your child. Keep trying, and over time, you'll find the methods and ideas that work best for your son or daughter.

Remember, you are not alone in this journey. With love, patience, and the right support, your child can thrive. Together, we can make a difference in their lives.

Chapter 2

Understanding Autism and the Diagnosis Process

As a parent, it's natural to worry about your child's development and behavior. However, not all parents know about Autism Spectrum Disorder (ASD). Before Jeremy's diagnosis, I didn't know much about ASD. I had heard of it, but I didn't understand what it really meant or how it could affect a child. This lack of knowledge is common among many parents.

Most of us learn about ASD through our own experiences or when someone points out that there might be something different about our child. Parents need to educate themselves about ASD and other developmental disorders. Understanding the signs and symptoms can help in recognizing if there might be a concern with your child's development.

Recognizing the Signs and Getting Help

As mentioned, if you are aware of some differences in behavior, to ease your mind, print the chart on symptoms and evaluate it against your child. Parents I spoke to told me they only knew when the child's school teacher told them. Currently, many parents send their children to school early, as in kindergarten, as early as three or four years old. These groups are normally in nursery classes. Age five to six kindergarten is to prepare children for formal education. Most kindergarten teachers nowadays are aware of ADHD, ASD, and other developmental issues. Teachers then advise parents to see a doctor and confirm any concerns.

At this point, parents who are both working may overlook the symptoms. So, if teachers already notice something different, you can do an assessment yourself first. Learn about the symptoms of ASD and ADHD. It's best to know both. The next step is to bring your child to a child psychiatrist, psychologist, or pediatric neurologist. You can bring them to any medical professional. They will interview you, discuss the symptoms you've noticed, and do an in-depth assessment or observation of your child's behavior.

For more information, visit reputable websites and resources. If you look through the questions, some questions only parents can answer. For example, how the child communicates, can he or she button their clothes on their own, can they eat independently, and so on.

Here are some common signs to look out for:

Difficulty Making Eye Contact: Children with ASD often avoid eye contact. They may look away or seem uninterested when someone is talking to them.

Not Responding to Their Name: A child with ASD might not respond when you call their name, even if they have normal hearing.

Limited Speech or Difficulty Speaking: Some children with ASD start speaking later than their peers. They might have a limited vocabulary or struggle to form sentences.

Repetitive Behaviours: Look for repetitive actions like hand-flapping, rocking, or spinning. These behaviors are common in children with ASD.

Difficulty with Social Interactions: Children with ASD may have trouble understanding social cues. They might not know how to interact with other children or understand how others are feeling.

Unusual Reactions to Sounds, Smells, or Textures: Sensory issues are common. A child with ASD might be very sensitive to certain sounds, smells, or textures. They might cover their ears at loud noises or refuse to wear certain clothes because of how they feel.

Fixation of Specific Interests: Children with ASD might have an intense interest in specific topics or objects. They may spend a lot of time talking about or playing with the same thing.

Difficulty Adapting to Changes: Routine is very important to children with ASD. They might get upset with changes in their schedule or environment.

Unusual Play: Instead of playing with toys in a typical way, children with ASD might line them up or focus on parts of the toys, like the wheels on a car.

These signs can vary greatly from one child to another. Some children may show many of these signs, while others may show only a few. It's important to remember that every child is unique, and ASD can look different in each one.

The current lifestyle of parents, with both working, means that grandparents or maids often take care of the child. Self-help skills like eating on their own and dressing up are most probably done by the family or caretakers. A mother once told me that she wasn't aware of how much of the listed criteria her son did not know, not because he didn't know, but because he was not allowed to do things by himself. My experience was similar. During assessments, I had to answer "no" to many questions. At age three, I hardly bought any clothing with buttons or zips. Even if I did, I helped Jeremy put them on.

Don't be overwhelmed. Use it as a guideline and work on it. You'll be surprised how much of the list your child can actually do by themselves.

Autism comes in different types, and understanding where your child fits can help you find the right support. Here's a simple way to look at it:

When Jeremy was assessed at age three, the doctors in Singapore categorized his autism as between mild and moderate. This was based on his behavior and skills at that time. For many questions during the assessment, I had to answer "no" because I wasn't sure if Jeremy could do certain things by himself. For example, I had always helped him with tasks like dressing, so I didn't know if he could manage buttons or zippers by his own.

There are generally three categories: mild, moderate, and severe autism.

Children with mild autism can usually talk and learn basic skills, but they might have trouble making friends and prefer routines. They might seem a bit different but can often go to regular schools with some help.

Children with moderate autism might have more noticeable problems with talking and socializing. They might use fewer words or gestures. They may also repeat certain behaviors and need more help with daily tasks. Special education and therapies can help them a lot.

Children with severe autism often have significant difficulties with talking and behavior. They might not talk at all or use very few words. They need a lot of support every day and benefit from intensive therapies. These children might attend specialized schools that understand their needs.

The doctors told me that as children grow, their abilities and needs become clearer. What seems like moderate autism at age three could change as the child develops. This is why regular check-ups and adjusting their support are important. The doctors advised using a list of developmental skills to train Jeremy. This approach helped us understand Jeremy's abilities better and know what he needed.

Understanding the different types of autism and where your child fits can guide you in finding the right resources and support. It also helps in setting realistic goals and expectations, making it easier to support your child as they grow.

Importance of Early Intervention Program (EIP)

An Early Intervention Program (EIP) can be very helpful for children with autism. These programs are designed to support young children and address their specific needs. Teachers in special needs schools often run these programs. They work with your child to understand their difficulties and help them improve.

One key part of EIP is Occupational Therapy (OT). This therapy focuses on helping children with activities that involve physical movements and thinking skills. OT can help with things like coordination, playing, learning, and daily tasks. For example, an occupational therapist might work with a child on skills like holding a pencil or playing with toys in a way that builds their abilities.

Another important part of EIP is Speech Therapy. This therapy helps children with communication. Speech therapists work with children to improve their ability to talk and express themselves. They also use other methods like picture cards to help children who have trouble speaking. The goal is for the child to be able to communicate their needs and interact with others as effectively as possible.

Early intervention is crucial because it provides children with the tools they need to develop and grow. The sooner a child starts receiving support, the better their progress can be. These programs help the child and teach parents how to support their child's development at home.

Role of Speech Therapy

Speech therapy plays an important role in helping children with autism communicate better. Communication isn't only about speaking. While many therapists work on helping children talk, they also focus on teaching other ways to communicate.

One effective method used is the Picture Exchange Communication System (PECS). This system allows children to use picture cards to express their needs and thoughts. For instance, if a child wants to drink water, they can use a card showing a picture of water. This method helps children express themselves without words, making communication easier for both the child and the caregiver.

Speech therapists also make sessions engaging by using toys, games, and fun activities. They may use tools like a toy kitchen to teach food-related words or a set of toy animals to teach animal names and sounds. These playful methods encourage children to participate and learn while having fun.

For children who struggle with pronouncing words, therapists help by focusing on specific sounds or practicing words step by step. They also use exercises to strengthen the muscles used in speaking, helping children improve their ability to form words clearly.

The main aim of speech therapy is to help children communicate in ways that are practical and meaningful. Whether through speaking or alternative methods, the goal is to help them express their needs, share their feelings, and interact with others comfortably.

It's also important to make therapy sessions enjoyable and not overwhelming. A positive and supportive environment, often filled with colorful toys and books, helps children feel comfortable and eager to learn.

Further details on specific techniques and benefits of speech therapy are explained in Chapter 4.

Chapter 3

Child Safety at Home and Outside for Autism

Safety is a big concern for every parent. We all want to keep our children safe, but can we always be safe? Accidents happen, and they're a natural part of life. However, when your child has autism, safety becomes even more critical.

Children with autism often don't understand danger the same way other kids do. They might not realize that touching a hot stove can burn them or that running into the street is dangerous. This means we need to be extra careful and always think about what could be risky for them.

I remember hearing about a parent who shared a moment when their child reached for a hot kettle without realizing it could hurt them. Thankfully, they were right there and managed to stop the child just in time, but it was a scary moment. Situations like this often happen with children who have autism because they don't always recognize what is safe and what isn't.

Everyday things in your home can become hazards. Furniture with sharp edges, small objects that can be swallowed, or unlocked cabinets with cleaning supplies can all pose risks. It's important to look at your home from your child's perspective and identify these dangers.

General Home Safety

Home safety is all about spotting things that could be dangerous for your child. Kids with autism often don't see danger the same way other kids do. They might not realize that something is hot or sharp, so it's up to us to notice these risks and do something about them.

Furniture Safety

First, let's talk about furniture. Look around your home and check where your furniture is placed and how stable it is. Sharp edges on tables or other pieces can be dangerous. If you have glass tables, think about replacing them or moving them out of reach.

I remember when Jeremy fell backward onto our glass-top coffee table. I had pushed it against the wall, but he still managed to fall on it. Thankfully, he wasn't hurt, but the glass cracked. After that, I replaced the top with wood to avoid any future accidents.

Here are some tips to make your furniture safer:

- **Secure Heavy Furniture:** Use wall anchors to secure big pieces like bookshelves and dressers. This stops them from tipping over if your child climbs on them.

- **Cover Sharp Corners:** Put corner protectors on sharp edges. They're easy to use and can prevent injuries if your child bumps into them.

- **Use Non-Slip Mats:** Place non-slip mats under rugs and in the bathroom to stop slips and falls. These mats help keep the rugs in place and provide extra grip.

Small Items and Choking Hazards

Small items can be a choking hazard. It's important to keep vthings that can easily be swallowed.

Here's how you can keep small items safe:

- **Store Small Items Safely:** Keep small items in locked cabinets or on high shelves where your child can't reach them.

- **Regular Checks:** Check the floor and low surfaces regularly for small items that might have been dropped or left behind.

- **Childproof Containers:** Use childproof containers for things that need to be accessible but safe, like medications or small craft supplies.

The kitchen is full of potential dangers, especially for children with autism. They might not realize that the stove is hot or that knives are sharp, so it's important to make this area as safe as possible.

One of the first things to do is to keep sharp objects out of reach. Store knives, scissors, and other sharp tools in high drawers or on shelves where your child can't get to them. If you need to use lower drawers, childproof locks are a great solution to keep them secure.

Cooking activities require extra attention. Always turn off the gas stove when you're not using it. Stove knob covers can help prevent your child from accidentally turning on the burners. And when you're cooking, it's important to supervise your child closely. Hot surfaces and boiling water can cause serious injuries, so keeping a close watch is essential.

Cleaning supplies can also be hazardous. These items are often poisonous if ingested, so it's crucial to keep them out of reach. Store all cleaning liquids and chemicals in a locked cabinet or on a high shelf. Using cabinet locks can help keep these dangerous items away from your child.

The bathroom can be a dangerous place for children they might not understand that water can be risky or that some items should not be touched.

First, it's important to keep water pails and other containers out of reach. Even a small amount of water can be dangerous. Store toiletries like creams, lotions, and mouthwash on high shelves or in locked cabinets. Cleaning supplies should also be stored safely, out of reach of children.

I remember one afternoon when Jeremy was playing while I decided to take a short nap on the sofa. I thought I could rest for just a few minutes. When I woke up, I noticed that the house was unusually quiet, and every parent knows that silence can mean trouble.

I quickly got up and started looking for him. I found him in the bathroom. There was an empty pail, and he had filled it with water. He had added everything he could find, the house keys, the TV remote, and even his slippers. He was sitting inside the pail, splashing and playing with bubbles, completely unaware of the mess he had made. This reminded me never to leave an empty pail in the bathroom, as children can easily fill it with water and create unexpected situations.

Seeing him like that made me realize how important it is to always keep an eye on him and to store things safely. I just had to buy a new remote.

To keep the bathroom safe:

- Use non-slip mats in the bathtub and on the bathroom floor to prevent slips and falls.

- Keep electrical items like hairdryers and razors unplugged and stored away after use. Water and electricity are a dangerous mix.

Traveling Safely

Traveling with a child who has autism can be challenging, but with some simple steps, you can make it much safer.

One of the first things to remember is the importance of securing your child in a car seat or with a seat belt. This is crucial for their safety.

I remember one time when we parked the car for just a few minutes to deliver something to a shop. When I came back, I found Jeremy had opened the car fragrance and was playing with the jelly inside. Luckily, none of it ended up in his mouth, but his curiosity could have put him in danger.

Training your child to use seat belts properly is also important. Jeremy was always buckled up in his toddler chair, but as he grew, I had to teach him to use the car seatbelt. It took some time and patience, but eventually, he got used to the routine. Now, as soon as he gets in the car, he buckles up without a fuss.

When you're out in public places, keeping an eye on your child is crucial. Children with autism can be unpredictable and might wander off.

One helpful tool is an anti-loss wrist bracelet. These bracelets connect your child to you with a stretchy cord. They are comfortable and come in different designs, so you can find one that suits your child. Some even come with a small lock to ensure it stays on. This helps prevent your child from running off and getting lost.

These bracelets give you peace of mind in crowded places like malls or parks. You can focus on what you're doing, knowing your child is right next to you. There are many options available online, and they are usually affordable. Some even come with built-in alarms that sound if the bracelet is tampered with. The alarm can also trigger if they move even slightly away, allowing you to take immediate action for their safety, especially if your child has a habit of wandering.

Another useful tool is an engraved information bracelet. These can include details like your child's name, "autism," and emergency contact numbers. If your child gets lost, this information can help people contact you quickly.

I remember a time when we were at the supermarket. I was paying at the cashier, and Jeremy was right next to me. In a split second, he disappeared. My heart raced as I frantically looked around. Luckily, it was a place we frequently visited, and the staff knew Jeremy. One of the salesgirls called out, "Madam, your son is over here." She had found him near the toy section, completely engrossed. That experience made me realize the importance of using safety tools.

General Safety Measures

First, take a good look around your home. Try to see it from your child's eyes. What might they find interesting but dangerous? Think about sharp corners, reachable cords, or open windows. It's important to identify these risks and address them.

Childproof locks are a great way to keep your child safe. Use these on doors and drawers to prevent your child from accessing dangerous items. Keeping laminated contact information cards handy is also a good idea. These can be placed in your child's backpack or pockets so that if they get lost, someone can contact you easily.

Installing sensors on doors is another helpful tip. These sensors can alert you if your child tries to leave the house or enter a room that might not be safe for them. It's a simple but effective way to keep track of their movements and ensure they stay in safe areas.

Designating a specific area for your child to play can make a big difference. This area should be free from hazards and filled with toys and activities they enjoy. It's important to let them have some freedom within these safe boundaries. Supervised freedom helps them explore and learn without constant worry.

Sibling Involvement and Additional Precautions

Involving siblings in safety measures can be very helpful. Brothers and sisters can play an important role in keeping a child with autism safe. Teaching siblings to watch out for each other, especially for their brother or sister with autism, adds an extra layer of safety and builds a sense of care and responsibility.

For example, older siblings can be taught what to watch for, like potential dangers that their brother or sister with autism might not recognize, especially in playgrounds. This could include things like running into the street, climbing too high, or touching something unsafe. By understanding these risks, siblings can be more aware and supportive.

A simple rule can be put in place, like asking the sibling to call an adult if they see something unsafe. This way, the sibling knows it's not their job to fix the situation but to let an adult know immediately. This reduces pressure on them while ensuring that the child with autism stays safe.

Another important thing is to keep spare keys accessible. I learned this the hard way when Jeremy locked himself in the bedroom once. Now, I keep a set of spare keys in a spot where I can quickly grab them if needed. This way, if he ever locks himself in again, I can get him out without any fuss.

It's also crucial to secure electrical appliances and wires. Jeremy loves to explore, and sometimes he finds his way to places he shouldn't be. Making sure that all electrical items are unplugged and stored away when not in use helps prevent accidents. I also use cord organizers to keep wires out of reach.

Creating a safe environment is about being proactive and making thoughtful changes.

It might seem like a lot at first, but these small steps can make your home a safer place for your child. And remember, every little bit helps in keeping them safe and giving you peace of mind.

Chapter 4

Finding the Right Schools and Therapists

Each child is unique, and finding the right combination of therapies and schools can significantly impact their development.

School plays a vital role in every child's life, and it's especially important for children with autism. School provides a structured environment where children can learn not only academic skills but also social and life skills that are essential for their development.

For children with autism, school offers a routine and consistency that can help them feel secure and understand what to expect each day. This structure is important because many children with autism thrive on routine and predictability.

Schools that specialize in supporting children with autism have trained staff who understand their unique needs. These teachers and therapists use specific strategies to help children learn and progress at their own pace. They provide a safe and nurturing environment where children can explore their abilities and gain confidence.

For parents, having their child in school provides valuable support and resources. Teachers often share insights and strategies that can be used at home, making it easier to support their child's learning and development outside of school.

Understanding your child starts with acting early. Early intervention works because it focuses on your child's brain while it's still growing and flexible. These therapies help your child now and build a strong base for learning and growing in the future.

I've seen firsthand how starting early can make a huge difference. It's about the therapies, and giving your child the best possible start. Every small achievement builds their confidence and helps them gain the skills they need to navigate the world more comfortably.

One of the ways this can be achieved is through Early Intervention Programs. These programs are designed to support young children with developmental delays or autism and typically start as early as two or three years old. They are often conducted by special needs schools and focus on providing children with the tools and strategies they need during their most formative years.

The early years are crucial because a child's brain is still developing and is more adaptable during this time. Starting intervention as soon as a diagnosis is made can make a significant difference. It allows therapists and parents to work together to build new skills and encourage positive behaviors. These efforts address immediate challenges and create a strong foundation for future growth. Every small step forward becomes part of a bigger journey, helping the child gain confidence and independence over time.

EIP programs are carefully designed to meet each child's unique needs and schedule. Therapists work closely with families to create plans that include activities aimed at improving communication, motor skills, and social interactions. This personalized approach helps ensure that each child is supported in a way that matches their abilities and needs.

Progress in these programs is not about reaching a final goal but about making steady improvements over time. The activities and focus areas are adjusted continuously as the child grows and develops new skills.

EIP is a journey that evolves with the child, focusing on consistent growth and helping them develop the skills they need step by step. It's about creating a strong foundation and adapting along the way to support the child's ongoing progress.

General Areas Covered by EIP

EIP covers a wide range of developmental areas, including:

- **Communication:** Helping children develop language skills, whether through spoken words, sign language, or picture exchange systems.

- **Gross Motor Skills:** Activities that improve large muscle movements, such as running, jumping, and climbing.

- **Fine Motor Skills:** Tasks that enhance small muscle movements, like writing, buttoning clothes, and using utensils.

- **Self-Care:** Teaching children to perform daily activities independently, such as dressing, eating, and brushing their teeth.

- **Social Skills:** Encouraging interaction with peers and adults, understanding social cues, and developing appropriate play behaviors.

Benefits Observed by Parents

Many parents have observed significant benefits from Early Intervention Programs (EIP). Here are a few key improvements:

Confidence: Children often become more confident as they learn new skills and achieve milestones. Parents have noted that their children feel more secure and capable as they progress through these programs.

Behavior: Early intervention helps manage and improve behaviors. Structured activities and consistent routines make a big difference in how children respond and adapt to their environment.

Positive Results: Overall development in areas like communication, motor skills, and social interactions often leads to noticeable improvements in a child's daily life.

The support provided by EIP doesn't end with the child, it extends to parents as well. The advice and strategies shared by teachers and therapists help parents build a strong foundation at home, ensuring consistency in the child's learning journey. As these skills develop, the next important step is finding the right school, a decision that plays an important role in shaping the child's progress and happiness.

Here are some important factors to consider when selecting a school:

Factors to Consider

- **Qualified and Well-Trained Teachers:** Teachers who are trained to work with children with autism can make a big difference. They understand the unique needs of these children and use specialized strategies to help them learn and grow. Look for schools with teachers who have experience and training in special education.

- **Not Overcrowded with Students:** Smaller class sizes are beneficial because they allow for more individualized attention. In a less crowded classroom, teachers can focus more on each child's needs, providing the support and guidance they require.

- **Ensuring the Child is Happy and Comfortable:** The right school is one where your child feels happy and comfortable. A positive school environment can help children feel more secure and open to learning. It's important to observe how your child reacts to the school environment and whether they seem content and engaged.

Choosing the right school for a child with special needs can sometimes take time and careful consideration. Not every school will be the right fit, and it might require some trial and error before finding a place where the child can thrive. Some schools may have larger class sizes, which can make it difficult for children who need more individualized attention or stimulation. In these cases, a child might lose focus or feel disconnected from the learning environment.

Specialized schools or smaller classrooms often provide better support. Teachers with experience in working with children with special needs can use personalized strategies to help the child learn and progress at their own pace. Smaller class sizes allow teachers to focus more on each child's specific needs, providing the right balance of structure, interaction, and stimulation.

I had to go through the same process before finding the right school for Jeremy.

Once the decision is made, it opens up another question, should the school be private or government-run? Each option comes with its own benefits and challenges, and understanding these differences is an important part of making the right choice.

Comparison Between Private and Government-run Schools

Choosing between private and government-run schools can be a tough decision. Each has its own set of advantages and challenges.

Private schools often provide smaller class sizes, which means teachers can give more attention to each child. With fewer students in a class, teachers can focus on understanding the individual needs of every child. Many private schools also offer programs specially designed for children with autism. These programs may include therapy sessions as part of the school day, helping children receive the support they need while continuing their education. This environment allows children to learn and grow at their own pace in a supportive setting.

Government-Run Schools

- **More Accessible:** Government schools are usually easier to find and cost less, making them an option for many families. In Malaysia, special needs children receive incentives from the government.

- **Inclusive Programs:** Some government schools include programs where children with different kinds of disability learn together. This helps children understand and interact with others who may be different from them.

- **Fewer Resources:** These schools often have bigger classes and less staff, which makes it harder for teachers to give each child personal attention. In some other countries, education for special needs children is free and follows a clear, well-organized plan.

Choosing the right school for a child with autism depends on many things. It's important to look for schools with skilled teachers, smaller class sizes, and a place where your child feels comfortable and happy. Every child is different, so what works for one child may not work for another. It's helpful to watch how your child adjusts, talk to the teachers, and be open to trying a different school if needed.

Note: This information reflects general trends and might vary by location. While private schools often have smaller class sizes and more resources, some government schools may also provide strong support through inclusive programs. Always research specific schools to find what fits best for the child's needs.

Finding the right school is an important part of supporting a child with autism, but it's not the only focus. Therapies like occupational therapy work alongside education to help children build essential skills for life.

Role of Occupational Therapy in Helping Children with Autism

Occupational therapy focuses on helping children with autism, develop essential skills needed for daily life. This includes areas like improving fine motor skills, enhancing sensory processing, and building social interaction abilities. The therapy aims to support their independence and participation in every day activities by addressing specific challenges and needs.

Focus on Improving Sensory Processing, and Self-Care Abilities

- **Sensory Processing:**

  o Children with autism often have sensory processing issues, where they may be overly sensitive to sounds, textures, lights, or other sensory inputs. OT helps them learn to manage and respond to these sensory inputs more effectively.

    Disclaimer: This topic is an important resource to help parents understand the sensory needs of a child. While it may not cover every aspect of autism, it provides valuable insights that can greatly support a child's upbringing.

  o **Sensory Diet:** A sensory diet is a personalized plan that includes activities designed to meet a child's sensory needs. It helps regulate their sensory system and improve their ability to focus and engage in daily activities.

- **Self-Care Abilities:**

  o OT helps children learn self-care tasks, such as dressing, grooming, and eating. These skills are critical for their independence and self-esteem.

Jeremy did go through all these training sessions. Since we started early, it had a positive impact on his progress.

Importance of Finding a Qualified Occupational Therapist

A good therapist will have experience working with children with autism and understand their unique needs. They will create a personalized plan for your child and provide one-on-one sessions to ensure that your child gets the most benefit from the therapy.

One-on-one sessions are essential because they allow the therapist to focus entirely on your child's needs. This personalized attention helps in identifying specific challenges and working on them effectively. *These are centres that provide only OT-related training.*

Finding the right occupational therapist is only one part of the process. Hearing about the experiences of other parents can provide valuable insights and inspiration. One such story is about Jack, a lively boy diagnosed with ADHD and some symptoms of autism. Jack's parents included Occupational Therapy (OT) as a key part of his routine to support his development.

Jack's daily schedule was well-structured. In the mornings, he attended a regular kindergarten, which gave him the chance to interact with children outside of a special needs program. This social exposure helped him learn from his peers and build social skills. After school, he would have lunch and a short rest at home, where he was cared for by his grandparents.

In the afternoons, Jack attended a special needs school. The smaller class sizes and tailored teaching methods allowed

Jack to receive the focused attention he needed. His teachers, trained in managing hyperactivity, used engaging techniques to keep him interested and learning.

Three times a week, Jack attended OT sessions, which were seamlessly integrated into his school schedule. These sessions focused on improving his motor skills and sensory processing, helping him develop better coordination and manage his energy levels. The OT sessions made a big difference, enabling Jack to participate more effectively in both school and home activities.

Occupational therapy focuses on helping children build essential life skills, while speech therapy works on improving how they communicate. Communication is how we connect, share, and understand each other. For children with autism, finding ways to express themselves and understand others can be a challenge. This is where speech therapy becomes so important.

Speech Therapy (ST)

Speech therapy is essential for helping children with autism improve their communication skills. Communication involves both expressing oneself and understanding others. Many children with autism face challenges in these areas, making speech and language development very important.

When Jeremy began speech therapy, it was clear how essential this support would be. Initially, Jeremy had a limited understanding of spoken words and vocabulary. He struggled to express his needs and often became frustrated when others couldn't understand him. Speech therapy aimed to bridge this gap by helping him develop his communication skills step by step.

Speech therapists use various methods to make learning engaging and effective. For example, they often use picture cards with images of everyday objects like a ball, a cup, or a cat. Children are encouraged to pick a card, and the therapist says the word while helping the child repeat it. This process helps them connect words to objects and actions, slowly building their vocabulary. One method commonly used is the ***Picture Exchange Communication System (PECS).*** This system uses visual symbols to help children with limited verbal skills communicate their needs and thoughts. PECS can guide children in expressing themselves, starting with basic requests and gradually expanding their ability to communicate more complex ideas.

Progress in speech therapy usually happens step by step. Initially, the focus might be on simple, everyday words like "eat," "water," "play," and "help." Once children are comfortable using single words, the therapist may introduce two-word phrases such as "want water" or "play ball." Gradually, this builds their confidence and ability to communicate.

A good speech therapist tailors each session to fit the child's needs and interests. Using activities that the child enjoys, like playing with favorite toys, makes learning more fun and engaging. For instance, if a child loves toy cars, the therapist might incorporate them into the session to teach new words and phrases.

Consistent practice at home is also very important. Therapists often suggest simple exercises that parents can do with their children, such as encouraging them to use words like "please," "more," or "thank you" during mealtime. Regular practice reinforces what is learned in therapy and helps the child use these skills in daily life.

Speech therapy also helps children with understanding and listening. Games are often used to teach them how to follow instructions and respond to questions. These activities can improve their listening skills and their ability to engage with others.

Many parents have seen how speech therapy helps their children progress. For example, Jack's story highlights how one-on-one sessions and engaging activities supported his development and communication skills.

Speech Therapy was another important part of Jack's routine. Once a week, a speech therapist would visit Jack at home for a one-on-one session. This personalized attention in a familiar environment made a significant impact on his communication skills.

The therapist used fun and interactive activities to make learning enjoyable. By incorporating games and engaging exercises, Jack stayed motivated and showed steady progress. The speech therapy sessions were tailored to Jack's unique needs, helping him gradually develop his ability to express himself and understand others better.

Jack's parents found that combining school with therapy sessions gave him the balance he needed to grow socially and academically. Speech therapy, in particular, helped Jack become more confident in his interactions, allowing him to connect with others in a meaningful way.

Each child's journey is different, but finding methods that allow them to communicate and connect can open up incredible possibilities. Another example of this is Naoki Higashida, which discusses the impact of finding the right tools and approaches to help children express themselves.

Naoki Higashida is an inspiring example of how the right support can make a big difference for children with autism. Born in Japan, Naoki is non-verbal, but he found a way to communicate using a simple alphabet grid. This tool helped him share his thoughts and feelings, something that was very difficult for him before.

Using this grid, Naoki was able to write a book called *The Reason I Jump* when he was just thirteen years old. The book gives a glimpse into what life is like for someone with autism, helping others understand the challenges and feelings he experiences. Naoki's story shows how important it is to find methods that work for each child, giving them a chance to express themselves and achieve things that might have seemed impossible.

Finding the right tools and methods can create new opportunities for children with autism. Every child is different, and their learning and therapy should reflect their individual needs. Many parents find that combining different environments, like regular and special schools along with therapy, creates a balanced approach that supports both social and developmental growth.

Parents choose to send their children to regular school for socialization and exposure while supplementing with therapy sessions in the afternoon. This approach helps children receive the benefits of both environments.

For example, some parents have noted that regular school sessions help their children learn to adapt to different social situations and develop routines. Therapy sessions, on the other hand, provide targeted support that addresses specific developmental needs. This combination ensures that children with autism receive a comprehensive education and therapy experience.

Professional and experienced guidance is crucial in this process. Teachers and therapists who understand the unique needs of children with autism can make a significant difference. They can provide the right support and strategies to help children progress and reach their potential.

Having the right teachers and therapists is important, but understanding specific approaches like behavior therapy can make an even bigger difference. Behavior therapy focuses on addressing challenges by understanding the reasons behind certain actions and guiding children toward more positive behaviors.

Understanding Behavior Therapy

Behavior therapy is a helpful approach to support children with autism in developing positive behaviors and managing challenging ones. This type of therapy focuses on understanding why certain behaviors occur and finding effective ways to address them. For example, aggressive behaviors like hitting, biting, or throwing objects might happen because the child feels frustrated or overwhelmed. Behavior therapy helps replace these actions with more positive behaviors through consistent practice and reinforcement.

A key part of behavior therapy is rewarding positive behavior. This involves recognizing and encouraging the child whenever they follow instructions or behave well. Rewards can be simple, like giving a sticker, extra playtime, or verbal praise. These rewards help children understand which behaviors are expected and appreciated, making them more likely to repeat those actions.

Challenges Faced by Parents in Managing Behavior Issues

Managing behavior issues can be a big challenge for parents. Aggressive behaviors, like hitting or biting, are often ways for children to express their emotions or cope with sensory overload. Addressing these behaviors effectively starts with understanding what causes them.

It plays a big role in identifying triggers and teaching strategies to handle difficult situations. Therapists might suggest calming techniques, like deep breathing or using a reassuring tone, to help the child feel more in control during moments of frustration. These methods can be very helpful in reducing meltdowns and other challenging behaviors.

Behavior therapy supports the child's development and gives parents practical tools to manage difficult moments. By identifying triggers and encouraging positive actions, families can create a more supportive environment that helps children grow and feel secure.

Behavior therapy helps children learn to manage their emotions and responses, but sometimes challenges go beyond behaviors and are linked to sensory processing.

If I were to give advice to other parents with autistic children, I would strongly recommend learning more about sensory processing. It's a topic that offers valuable insights and perspectives, helping you understand your child better and choose the right approaches. Often, we overlook this area, but understanding it can make a big difference in supporting your child's needs.

Sensory Processing Disorder (SPD)

Sensory Processing Disorder (SPD) happens when the brain struggles to process and respond to sensory information. This can affect any of the senses, including sight, sound, touch, taste, and smell, as well as movement and body position. Many children with autism experience sensory challenges, and this can have a big impact on their behavior.

For instance, a child with SPD might be overly sensitive to loud noises, which can cause anxiety or meltdowns in busy or noisy places. On the other hand, some children may be under-responsive and actively seek intense sensory input, like spinning in circles or bumping into objects.

These sensory issues can affect daily routines in unexpected ways. Certain textures in clothing, for example, might feel uncomfortable and cause distress. It can make getting dressed a difficult task. Similarly, loud sounds, like a blender or vacuum cleaner, might feel unbearable, leading to strong reactions.

Understanding these sensory triggers is an important step in managing behavior and creating a supportive environment. Simple changes, like using noise-canceling headphones in loud places or choosing soft, tag-free clothing, can make a big difference. Sensory-friendly adjustments can help children feel more comfortable and reduce their stress.

For children with oral sensory needs, therapists often recommend safe items to chew, such as crunchy vegetables or sensory chew toys. These options help meet their sensory needs in a safe and manageable way.

Managing sensory challenges takes time and learning. Recognizing what causes discomfort and making thoughtful adjustments can significantly improve a child's daily experiences. With the right support and strategies, progress becomes visible, bringing ease and comfort to both parents and children.

By addressing these sensory challenges, we noticed improvements in Jeremy's behavior and overall well-being. It was a continuous learning process, but each small step made a big difference in making life more manageable and fulfilling.

Chapter 5

Building a Routine and Managing Family Life

By now, you've already taken some important steps. You've understood your child's diagnosis, made your home a safer place, and found the right schools and therapy centers that meet your child's needs. You've worked hard to get here, making sure everything is in place for your child's growth.

But now, with these things set up, you might be asking yourself: **What should I do next?**

Your child spends a lot of time at home, outside of school and therapy sessions. To make sure they continue to progress, it's important to set some clear rules and routines that everyone in the family can follow. These rules help keep your child engaged and support the work being done in their Early Intervention Program (EIP), Occupational Therapy (OT), Speech Therapy (ST), and Behavior Therapy (BT) sessions.

Having everyone in the family involved is key. When the whole family follows the same rules and routines, it creates a consistent environment for your child. This consistency helps them understand what is expected of them, which in turn supports their development.

One of the first things you might consider is rearranging your home routine to include some of these new rules. For example, if your child's Early Intervention Program (EIP) school has a routine where after meals, children are taught to take their plate, put it in the sink, wash it, clean it, and leave it to dry, you can implement the same routine at home. This kind of repetition helps reinforce the skills they are learning at school.

Another example might be the way your child eats. If they are being trained to eat with a fork and spoon during Occupational Therapy (OT) sessions, it's important to continue this practice at home. Consistency in these small but important routines can make a big difference in how well your child adapts and learns.

But for these routines to be truly effective, everyone in the household needs to be on the same page. If one family member finishes their meal and leaves their plate in the sink without washing it, it becomes challenging to ask your child with autism to wash their plate. Children with autism are very observant. They might think, "Why should I wash my plate when others don't?" This is why setting a routine that everyone follows is so important.

The same goes for using utensils. In many Asian families, it's common to eat with hand, which is perfectly fine. But if you want your child to learn to eat with a fork and spoon, everyone in the family must use utensils consistently. If some family members use their hands while others use utensils, it can confuse your child and make it harder for them to learn.

You might have noticed that your child follows rules well at school but struggles to do the same at home. This is because schools usually have clear, consistent rules that everyone follows. It's helpful to talk to your child's teachers and understand how they manage routines at school. You can then try to incorporate similar practices at home, ensuring that everyone in the family sticks to these routines.

It's also important to set an example in other areas. For instance, if you decide to limit sweets and junk food because your child is hyperactive, then no one in the family should be eating these foods around them.

Children with autism are keen observers. They may not always express what they notice right away, but they are always watching and learning from the people around them. Sometimes, it's easy to think that because they might take longer to understand or respond, they're not picking up on what's happening. But in reality, they are absorbing so much more than we might realize.

This is why it's so important to be mindful of the behaviors we model. Children with autism are smart, they might not always show it in the typical ways, but they're processing and learning from the environment around them.

Let me tell you about Mrs. Nadia. She has four daughters, and after years of waiting, she was finally blessed with a son, Nasir. But by the time Nasir turned three, he was diagnosed with autism. You can imagine how heartbroken and sad they were to learn that their only son had autism. It was a difficult moment for the family, especially for Mrs. Nadia, who had to gather her four daughters and explain to them what autism was and what it meant for their brother.

Her daughters were all of different ages, so it wasn't easy to make them understand. But the first rule Mrs. Nadia set was clear: whenever she introduced a rule, everyone had to follow it. And not just follow it, but also practice it regularly, especially with Nasir. The youngest of the girls was only three years older than Nasir, so Mrs. Nadia made sure that both of them did their table tasks or homework together. This way, Nasir was never alone in what he was doing.

Every time the two older sisters came home from school or classes, they would use their free time to help Nasir learn some fine motor skills. They would sit with him, practicing together, turning what could have been a solitary task into a shared activity. Mrs. Nadia often told me that even though it was painful to know that Nasir had autism, she felt blessed to have four daughters who were so willing to help out in their own ways, each contributing to Nasir's growth.

But even with all the support, there were moments that showed just how quickly a child with autism can pick up on the smallest changes in routine. There was this one time when the eldest sister, Emma, was in a rush to get to her tuition class. She came home from school, left her shoes at the doorstep instead of putting them on the shoe rack, and quickly changed into her slippers before heading out the door.

That one small break in routine had a surprising impact. Nasir, seeing his sister leave her shoes by the door, must have thought, "That's easier than putting them on the rack." From that day on, he started leaving his shoes at the doorstep too, just like Emma had done that one time. It was one of those moments that made Mrs. Nadia realize just how quickly a child can learn from what they see, even if it's something they only see once.

This situation really made her wonder. How is it that a single instance of breaking a rule can stick so quickly, while the family's long efforts to establish and follow rules seem to take so much longer? To get things back on track, Mrs. Nadia made sure that Emma placed her shoes on the rack and had Nasir do it with her for the next week. Slowly, Nasir started following the rules again, putting his shoes on the rack just like before.

Rules need to be followed by everyone, all the time.

Most of the time, the main provider for the family is the dad, while the mom takes on the role of caregiver. This often means that mothers are the ones handling everything related to the child's needs, whether it's sending them to school, taking them to therapy, or managing their daily routines at home. And let's not forget the household chores that need to be done as well. It can all add up, and it can be overwhelming when one person is trying to juggle so many responsibilities.

If you can afford to hire a maid or helper to take on some of these tasks, it can really lighten the load. Having someone to help with the housework or even assist with your child's needs can take a huge burden off your shoulders. But if that's not an option, it's important to reach out to your family for support. Talk to your husband, siblings, or close relatives. See if there's anything they can do to help, whether it's taking on certain tasks or giving you a break when you need it.

Even if your husband is busy with work, maybe he can take on some responsibilities during his days off. This small shift can give you a much-needed break and help reduce the stress and exhaustion that come with being the primary caregiver. Remember, caring for a special needs child is a long-term commitment. If you try to do everything on your own, there's a risk of burning out, feeling overwhelmed, and struggling with stress and anxiety.

It's crucial to take breaks and find time for yourself. Whether it's going out for a cup of tea with a friend, catching a movie, or just doing something you love but haven't had time for, you need to make space for *"me time."* I know this from personal experience. There was a point when I felt like I couldn't think straight anymore, my mind was so full that I couldn't solve even the smallest challenges.

My sister noticed this and pushed me to go on a two-night, three-day retreat. It was just what I needed. I met new people, participated in group activities, and for the first time in a long while, I focused solely on enjoying myself. By the end of the retreat, I felt lighter, my head was clear, and I was ready to return to my routine, only this time, I felt different. I was happier, more relaxed, and full of energy.

It's your body's way of telling you to slow down and recharge. Don't worry, taking that much-needed break won't cause any major issues at home. It might just be the thing you need to come back stronger and more prepared to handle whatever comes your way.

Throughout these 18 years with Jeremy, I've met and talked to many parents, each with their own experiences and challenges. Two parents, Mrs. Uma and Mrs. Chan, shared their stories with me, and they really made me think about the journey we're all on.

Mrs. Uma has two sons, with a ten-year age gap between them. Her second son was diagnosed with autism. We were talking one day, and I mentioned how I felt like there was just so much to do and not enough time to get everything done. At that point, Jeremy was about three or four years old, and I was feeling overwhelmed.

Mrs. Uma told me about her daily routine. She wakes up very early in the morning to finish her household chores, and then she focuses on her son's needs, taking him to school, and therapy, and continuing his training at home. I couldn't help but wonder why I couldn't manage things the way she did. So, I tried to change my routine to be more like hers. I pushed myself to handle everything on my own.

But after two weeks, I got really sick. It took me a week to recover, and during that time, no one was able to follow up with Jeremy's routine, other than sending him to school and therapy. When I finally got back to our routine, Jeremy didn't cooperate the way he used to. He had already gotten used to the break from our structure, and it was hard to get back on track.

That's when I realized something important: it's not helpful to compare yourself to other mothers or caregivers. Each of us is unique and has our own way of doing things. What matters most is that we do our best and take care of ourselves, too. Your health is important because you need to be strong for your child.

Two years later, I saw Mrs. Uma again. She had moved overseas with her husband and had just returned home. When I saw her, I was surprised at how much she had changed. She looked very thin and tired, and even though she told me she was okay, it was clear that she wasn't. The good news was that her son had made great progress. But seeing her made me think, should we sacrifice our own health just to see results? It's important to take care of ourselves while we take care of our kids.

Then there's Mrs. Chan. I met her while waiting for Jeremy's speech therapy class. Mrs. Chan was always well-dressed, calm, and happy. Her son, Sean, sat quietly beside her, following her instructions without any fuss. I was surprised when she told me that Sean had autism, just like Jeremy. I asked her how she managed to keep Sean so calm.

Mrs. Chan explained that Sean had been very hyperactive when he was three or four years old, just like Jeremy. She felt overwhelmed with everything she needed to do for him, so she decided to get help. Her husband is a businessman, so they were able to hire two maids, one to help with the household chores and another to help manage Sean. This made things much easier for her. She spent her time reading and researching what was best for Sean and took the maid to all the therapy sessions so that the maid could continue the training at home when she was busy.

She also changed Sean's diet and trained the other maid to cook meals that were suitable for him. With this extra help, Mrs. Chan was able to find time for herself, which allowed her to stay calm and focused. Sean was constantly receiving training, both at school and at home, and it made a big difference in his behavior and progress.

The key is finding a balance that works for you, so you can take care of your child while also taking care of yourself. Not everyone can afford to hire two maids, as finances can be a challenge. Instead, consider finding ways to manage with the help of those around you.

Chapter 6

Understanding and Managing Behavior Issues

Managing behavior issues is one of the biggest challenges parents of children with autism face. For many of us, getting the right support, like from an ABA (Applied Behavior Analysis) therapist, isn't always possible. Long waiting lists and limited access can make it difficult to get the help we need.

In my own experience, I couldn't always access the full support of an ABA therapist, but I found bits of guidance from Jeremy's teachers and occupational therapists that helped me along the way. I realized that while we might not have all the resources we need, we can still make a difference by applying what we can learn and adapting it to our own situation.

Other parents have shown me that it's possible to make things work, even if it's not perfect. They've taken the principles of ABA, learned the techniques on their own, and adjusted them to fit their homes and their children's needs. The main thing is setting clear rules and sticking to them, making sure that your child understands and follows these rules consistently.

Understanding the difference between a tantrum and a meltdown is really important. A tantrum is usually when a child wants something and will cry, shout, or act out until they get it. Once they get what they want, the behavior stops almost immediately. It's like they were putting on a show just to get what they needed.

A meltdown, though, is different. It doesn't stop even if you try to give them what they want. It's not about wanting something specific, it's about feeling overwhelmed, confused, or distressed. The child might not even know why they're upset, which makes it harder for them to calm down.

So, when you see your child going through something similar, you might start to wonder: Is this a tantrum, or is it a meltdown?

For children with autism, communication can be difficult, and that often leads to meltdowns. They might cry, walk back and forth, sit down and kick their legs. It's their way of expressing that something is really wrong, even if they can't put it into words.

Sometimes, Jeremy would throw things when he had a meltdown. I started noticing that this often happened when his routine was disrupted. In the early days, these meltdowns were quite common. I remember one time when I took Jeremy to his swimming class, which he absolutely loved. He was about four or five years old at the time. Just as we arrived, it started raining, and the coach had to cancel the class.

Jeremy couldn't understand why the class was canceled. We tried to show him the rain, pointing to the sky, but it didn't make sense to him. He didn't get why something he was so excited about was suddenly not happening. He began crying and showing signs of stress. In moments like this, trying to explain things to him was impossible, he just couldn't process it.

Even giving him his favorite toy didn't help because, in his mind, all that mattered was that he couldn't go swimming. This is what makes meltdowns so challenging, there are often many different reasons that can trigger them, especially when a child doesn't understand why something is happening. As a parent, I found myself trying to figure out what was causing these meltdowns.

I learned to look back and think about what happened just before the meltdown started. Sometimes, I could spot something that triggered it. Understanding the cause made it easier to avoid similar situations in the future. But at the moment, during a meltdown, it's impossible to reason with your child, they're just too overwhelmed.

I started keeping notes on Jeremy's behavior, especially when something didn't seem to add up. I'd talk to his teachers or therapists to get their perspective and see if I missed anything.

Staying calm was the best thing I could do. It wasn't about fixing things right then, but about understanding what led up to the meltdown so I could try to prevent it from happening again.

When I first started attending classes and talks to learn more about autism, one theory that was mentioned almost everywhere was the iceberg theory. At first, I didn't fully understand it, but over time, it became clear why it was such a common explanation.

The iceberg theory explains that what we see in a child with autism is just the tip of the iceberg. People often notice the visible traits, things like being well-behaved, compliant, hardworking, or even gifted. These are the qualities that are obvious to teachers, friends, or others who interact with the child briefly. They might say, *"Your child seems so good and quiet,"* because they only see what's on the surface.

However, the larger part of the iceberg is hidden beneath the water. This hidden part represents the struggles that aren't immediately visible. Social confusion, for example, when a child finds it difficult to understand how to connect with others. Sensory overload is another challenge, where bright lights, loud noises, or certain textures can feel overwhelming. There's also the feeling of being different, which can lead to frustration and exhaustion. Communication difficulties often make it hard for children with autism to express what they need or how they feel, even though they have so much happening internally.

Understanding this theory helps us see the bigger picture. It reminds us that what we observe is only a small part of what the child is going through. The visible behaviors or strengths are just one side, but there's a whole other world beneath the surface that requires patience and understanding. This theory highlights the importance of looking beyond appearances and acknowledging the challenges that may not be obvious.

As I learned more about autism, I came across something called flight risk. Many parents of children with autism deal with this. Sometimes, children with autism react strongly to what's happening around them. This can cause what is known as a "fight-or-flight" response. Their brain becomes very reactive and overstimulated, and they act on impulse.

When this happens, they might run away from something that frightens them or move quickly toward something that interests them. This behavior isn't always intentional. It's often an instinctive reaction. They may not even realize the risks involved, and this can make things challenging for parents.

Flight risk can happen anywhere, at home, in school, or outside. It could be triggered by loud sounds, bright lights, or sudden changes in their environment. Sometimes, it happens because something fascinates them, like a certain sound or object. Since they can't always explain why they are reacting this way, it's important for those around them to understand and be prepared.

Preventing and reducing meltdowns is something many parents of children with ASD find challenging. It's not always clear what triggers a meltdown, unlike a tantrum, where the cause is usually obvious. With a tantrum, you often know what the child wants, and once they get it, the behavior stops. But a meltdown is different, it can come out of nowhere, and as a parent, you're left trying to figure out what caused it.

One of the first steps in managing meltdowns is to analyze what might have triggered them. This takes time and observation. Parents need to be detectives, looking closely at what happened before the meltdown began. Was there a change in routine? Did something unexpected happen?

Understanding these triggers can help in avoiding similar situations in the future.

For Jeremy, certain tools helped him calm down during a meltdown. He found comfort in simple things like a handkerchief, ribbons, or strings, which he would flip back and forth to soothe himself. He also used to chew on the edge of a small towel, and having his favorite toy nearby often made a difference. The key was finding something that worked for him, something safe that he could use to calm himself down.

Every child is different, so it's about discovering what helps your child. It could be a particular object, a certain texture, or even a quiet space where they can go to calm down. Over time, with the right guidance, children can learn to manage their meltdowns better. As they grow older and begin to understand what's happening, they might even start to calm themselves down during a meltdown.

In Jeremy's case, as he grew up and learned how to manage his feelings, the frequency and intensity of his meltdowns decreased. It's a process that takes patience and consistency, but with time, it does get easier.

The important thing is not to give up and to keep trying different strategies until you find what works for your child.

Tantrums are often easier to spot in typical children. We've all seen it happen, like in a shopping mall when a child wants a toy or a sweet, and the parents say no. The child might start yelling, crying, or even drop to the floor, trying to get their way. It's an embarrassing situation for parents, and sometimes, to avoid the scene, they give in and buy what the child wants.

But doing that usually means you'll face the same situation again in the future. If you give in once, the child learns that throwing a tantrum works to get what they want.

It's important for parents to stand their ground. If the answer is no, it should stay no. But this doesn't mean you have to be harsh. You can explain to the child why they can't have what they want, in a loving and calm way. Giving in because of a tantrum sets a bad example and shifts the control from the parent to the child.

When it comes to children with ASD, it can be challenging to figure out whether a behavior is a tantrum or a meltdown. It's crucial to understand the reason behind the behavior before reacting. A tantrum can often be about seeking attention. The child might act out because they know it will make the parents focus on them. Understanding why the tantrum is happening helps in managing it better. You can then decide which behaviors are okay and which ones need to be addressed.

While tantrums can usually be managed by setting clear boundaries, meltdowns are a different story. But understanding the root of the behavior is the first step in handling both situations effectively.

This is where ABA (Applied Behavior Analysis) comes in. ABA offers ways to help manage and reduce tantrums in children with ASD. When Jeremy was younger, I didn't have access to a behavior therapist, so I often relied on advice from his occupational therapists (OT) and teachers. However, having a behavior therapist or psychologist can be really helpful in teaching children how to change negative behaviors into positive ones.

Sensory problems can often be behind some of the behaviors you see. Many behaviors might be because the child is either getting too much or too little stimulation from their environment. By addressing these sensory challenges, you might notice an improvement in behavior.

For children who are non-verbal, behavior is often their way of communicating. They might show negative behaviors because they're uncomfortable, upset, or confused. This is why it's so important to address these behaviors early on, before they become more ingrained.

When it comes to setting rules and disciplining with care, how you talk to your child really matters. Instead of saying "no" or "stop" all the time, you can try using more positive language. For example, instead of saying "don't run," you could say "let's walk together." Or instead of "stop shouting," you could say "use your quiet voice." These small changes in how you communicate can make a big difference in helping your child understand and follow the rules.

Have you ever noticed that you might manage your child better when the other parent isn't around?

There's another type of behavior that children often pick up at home, sometimes without us even realizing it. Many mothers or caregivers set up clear rules for the child to follow, often based on advice from teachers and therapists, and stick to them without fail.

But then, when dad comes home after a long day at work, he might be too tired to keep up with these rules. The child, excited to see their dad, may act differently, wanting to spend time freely without the usual structure. It's common for children not to listen as much to their mother when their father is around. Children also learn behaviors from others they see at school or in public places. They see how others act and sometimes pick up habits without us noticing.

If these new behaviors are not positive, they need to be addressed. It's important to have consistent rules so the child doesn't get confused by different expectations from each parent. Both parents need to be on the same page. It's important that dads don't break the rules either because it sends mixed signals. It might make the child think that mom's rules are too strict, while dad's approach is more fun. One way to avoid this is for parents to do activities together that both have agreed on, so the child sees that both parents are united in their approach.

Another point to consider is how parents handle disagreements. It's natural for couples to have their differences, but it's best not to argue or confront each other in front of the child. Children, even if they don't fully understand what's happening, can pick up on the negative energy. It's better to keep these discussions private, away from the kids. This applies to all children, not just those with autism.

Parenting: Then and Now

I remember how my own parents handled disagreements. My siblings and I could sense when something was off between them, but they never argued in front of us. We just noticed that they would stop talking to each other for a while, but life went on as usual. My mother would still prepare meals and call us to the table, just like always.

This was the usual routine in my house when I was growing up. Whenever my parents had a misunderstanding, my mom would ask me to tell my dad, "Girl, can you tell your dad that breakfast is ready?" From that, we knew something wasn't quite right between them. But as kids, we never knew what the issue was.

The same thing would happen at lunch. My mom would say, "Tell your dad that lunch is ready." By the time tea time came, which was a big thing in our house, things would start to change. Instead of asking me to tell my dad, she would call out to everyone, "Tea is ready. Come, everybody, let's have tea together." That's when we knew my mom was feeling better, and my dad would take it as a sign to head to the kitchen.

In the kitchen, we could hear them talking, but it was always in low voices, like they were discussing something important. My siblings and I were curious, but if we tried to go into the kitchen, they'd quickly tell us, "What are you doing? Go play in the hall with your sister." We knew to stay out of the way when they were having these quiet talks.

Normally, my dad wasn't home much, but on these days, when there was some disagreement, he'd stay home the whole day. It was another sign that something was going on. We could feel the tension, but we didn't know the details.

As the day went on, things would slowly go back to normal. By dinner time, the issue was usually resolved. My mom would announce, "Dinner is ready. Come, everybody, let's eat together." She'd even make a special effort to invite my dad, "Come, dear, let's have dinner as a family." That's how we knew everything was okay again.

The next morning, everything would be back to normal. The routine would continue like nothing had happened, and life would go on as usual.

Parenting back then was definitely different from how it is today. When I look back, I sometimes laugh at how my parents handled things. They had their own way of solving problems without us ever really knowing what was going on. And one thing that stands out to me is how my parents never used harsh or vulgar language, even when they were upset with us.

When we made mistakes, my dad or mom would scold us, but it was always about the mistake itself. They never used offensive words. Nowadays, it seems like those kinds of words are common in many homes, but in our house growing up, that just wasn't the case. The scolding was focused on what we did wrong, without any extra harsh words thrown in.

Today, things feel different. I live in a terrace house now, and even with all the doors and windows closed, I can sometimes hear what's going on in my neighbor's house. It's not like when I was growing up. Back then, even if something serious was happening next door, you wouldn't know about it because people were more private.

Kids today, whether they have ASD or not, are watching their parents closely. They learn from everything we do. And if you have a child with ASD, it adds another layer of challenge. Taking care of a special needs child is already demanding, and when you add in the pressures of family life, it can be overwhelming.

We're all human, and we all make mistakes. No one is perfect. But in front of your child, especially if they have special needs, it's important to try not to show any conflict. Behind closed doors, you can say what you need to each other, but it's best not to do it in front of the child. A normal child might think logically and conclude, "That's their problem, I'm not going to get involved," but a child with special needs might approach the situation differently.

It's hard to tell a child that certain behavior is wrong if they've seen it at home. They're learning from what they see. So, it's important to try to keep any misunderstandings or arguments out of sight.

This helps in creating a stable and peaceful environment, which is especially important for children who are already dealing with the challenges of ASD.

When you have a child with ASD and other children who don't, it's important to think about how you're balancing your time and attention. As parents, it's easy to focus so much on the needs of the child with ASD, especially given all the challenges that come with it. But in doing that, sometimes the other children in the family can feel left out or overlooked.

These other children also need your time, love, and attention. They are just as much a part of the family and have their own needs and feelings. I've seen families where this balance was a struggle, and it's something that really made me think. It's so important to spend time together as a family and make sure the siblings of the ASD child don't feel like they're being forgotten.

If a parent is always focused on the child with ASD and doesn't spend time with the other children, it can create a gap between the siblings. This can lead to the other children feeling sad or frustrated because they aren't getting as much attention.

It's important to keep this in mind and make an effort to include the other children in family time. They need to feel that they are also important, even if they don't have the same challenges as their sibling with ASD. This way, the family can stay connected, and everyone can feel loved and supported.

There's a family I know where the grandparents played a big role in helping with the children, especially since both parents were working. They were the ones who took care of the firstborn, Amina, making sure she got to and from kindergarten. Amina was a happy child who loved going to school, and everything seemed to be going well.

But then, the family welcomed their second daughter, Mira, who had special needs. As you might expect, everyone's attention naturally shifted to Mira. The grandparents, who were already involved in Amina's life, now had to focus more on Mira, taking her to her therapy sessions and making sure she got the care she needed.

For a while, things seemed okay. Amina continued to go to kindergarten, but slowly, her behavior started to change. The teachers noticed that Amina, who was usually sweet and well-behaved, began acting out. She started throwing tantrums over small things, becoming possessive of her toys, and even speaking rudely to her classmates. This was unusual for her, and it worried the teachers.

One day, when her grandfather went to pick her up from school, the teacher mentioned these changes to him. He was surprised because Amina had always been such a kind and easygoing child. Concerned, he gently asked her what was going on.

Amina's response revealed a lot. She said, in a hurt and frustrated voice, "Why do you want to correct me? Everyone spends all their time with Mira. It's okay, I can take care of myself."

This response made it clear that Amina was feeling left out. With so much attention being given to Mira, Amina felt like she was no longer important. Her acting out at school was her way of trying to get the attention she was missing at home.

Realizing this, the grandfather decided to spend more time with Amina, making sure she knew she was still loved and valued. He also talked to Amina's parents, encouraging them to do the same. It was a reminder that while Mira needed extra care, Amina still needed her share of attention and love too. When there's a child with special needs in the family, it's easy for the other children to feel overlooked.

It's important to make sure that the other children in the family, the ones without special needs, also feel cared for and included. While parents might spend a lot of time explaining what autism is and why their sibling needs more help, it's just as important that these other children feel noticed and loved.

These kids might have their own things they want to talk about or needs they want met, and they need to know that their parents are there for them too. Finding time for everyone to come together as a family helps the other children see that even though one sibling might need extra support, their parents still care deeply about them too.

When a child with ASD has siblings, it's all about finding that balance. The other children need to feel that, despite the extra care their sibling requires, they are just as loved and valued.

Every child in the family should feel like they matter.

Chapter 7

The GFCF Diet – What It Is and How It Helps

What is gluten?

Gluten is a protein that's naturally found in grains such as wheat, barley, and rye. It acts like a glue that holds food together and gives dough its elasticity, making things like bread soft and chewy. It's not only found in obvious foods like bread and pasta, but also in unexpected places like sauces, soups, or even processed foods where gluten is used as a thickener.

For many children with autism, gluten might be difficult to digest properly. The idea is that some children's bodies don't fully break down gluten, which could potentially lead to discomfort in the digestive system. This discomfort can sometimes be subtle, like stomach aches or bloating, but for other children, it might be more noticeable and show up as changes in their behavior.

Parents who have experimented with removing gluten from their child's diet have shared various positive outcomes. Some have reported improvements in their child's mood or attention, while others have noticed a reduction in behaviors like irritability or restlessness. It's important to note that not all children with autism will have issues with gluten. Each child is different, and it's always a good idea to consult with a healthcare professional before making significant changes to your child's diet.

What is casein?

Casein is a protein found in milk and dairy products like cheese, yogurt, and cream. It plays a big role in giving dairy its texture, particularly in products like cheese, where it helps create that stretchy, melty consistency. While most people digest casein without issues, some children with autism may struggle with it.

For certain children, casein might not be fully broken down in the body, which could lead to digestive discomfort, like bloating or stomach pain. Similar to gluten, some parents believe that casein can also affect behavior. They've observed that when dairy is removed from their child's diet, there's an improvement in mood, attention, or even physical comfort.

It's important to note, though, that not all children with autism have trouble digesting casein, and each child's response to it is different. For those who do experience issues, taking dairy out of the diet has helped them feel better and more settled.

Why the GFCF Diet?

The GFCF (Gluten-Free, Casein-Free) diet is based on the idea that removing gluten and casein from a child's meals might help with digestive issues or discomfort that could be impacting their behavior. For some children with autism, these proteins may not break down completely in the body, leading to problems such as bloating, stomach pain, or even affecting mood and attention.

Although research on the GFCF diet is still developing, some parents have reported seeing improvements in their child's comfort and behavior after removing gluten and dairy from their meals. The theory behind this is that incomplete digestion of gluten and casein can produce substances that may trigger reactions in sensitive children. These reactions can range from physical discomfort to changes in how the child interacts or focuses.

Transitioning to a GFCF Diet

Making the shift from a regular diet to a gluten-free, casein-free (GFCF) diet can be quite challenging, especially for parents who are just beginning to understand what foods contain gluten and casein. It's important to start by familiarizing yourself with the everyday foods that contain gluten. Once you have a clear understanding of which foods in your kitchen have gluten, you'll be better prepared to make changes.

Earlier in Chapter 5, I mentioned Mrs. Chan and her experience transitioning her son, Sean, to a GFCF diet. She shared how positive the results were once they followed the diet consistently. In the beginning, she spent a lot of time in the supermarket, carefully reading labels to find products that didn't contain gluten or casein. This process took effort, but over time, she became more comfortable identifying which foods were safe for her son.

A surprising challenge she faced was realizing how many of the sauces used in traditional Chinese cooking contained gluten. Soy sauce, for example, typically has gluten, but there are gluten-free alternatives available. Mrs. Chan found GFCF-specific stores and online shops that offered these alternatives, making the transition a bit easier.

Personally, I'm lucky because Indian cooking relies heavily on spices, which naturally don't contain gluten. I simply needed to cut out any flour-based items that contained gluten. However, I have to admit that I haven't fully committed to the GFCF diet for Jeremy. Instead, I test certain foods and monitor how they affect his behavior to see if there's any noticeable difference.

Some foods, even if they're gluten-free and casein-free, still cause Jeremy digestive problems. For example, I've tried cooking different kinds of meat, but they just don't sit well with his stomach. So, I've completely stopped cooking red meat for him. Jeremy can only eat chicken and fish without any issues. Any red meat tends to cause digestion problems for him. That's how I've figured out what works and what doesn't for his meals, and now everyone at home follows the same list.

One of the benefits of living in Malaysia is that we have such a diverse range of foods from different ethnic communities, Malay, Chinese, Indian, and others. Some parents I've spoken to shared how they gave up on the GFCF diet because they just didn't know what to cook anymore after cutting so many dishes from their usual meals. That's why I believe it's better to take things step by step. Start with the meals you already cook, and slowly add in new dishes from other communities.

Mrs. Chan, who is Chinese, faced difficulties adjusting her family's meals to suit her son's gluten-free diet. Many of her usual dishes relied on sauces with gluten, like soy sauce. To make things work, she started including Malay and Indian dishes in her cooking and found gluten-free alternatives for the sauces. Over time, she created a variety of meals that her son enjoyed, and the whole family could share together.

Eating out with a gluten-free diet can also be tricky. In Malaysia, there aren't many restaurants with clear gluten-free options, so parents like Mrs. Chan and I often have to look closely at menus and choose carefully to find something suitable. Though it takes some effort, it's worth it to make sure the child has safe and enjoyable meals.

Aside from gluten, another important change parents can make is to reduce sugar and avoid foods high in sugar content. It's an extra step, but it can make a big difference in managing your child's diet and overall well-being.

Those with ASD and ADHD have strong preferences when it comes to food. Jeremy, used to only eat crunchy vegetables like broccoli, cauliflower, and beans. I ended up cooking the same thing over and over, and I have to admit, it became tiring at times. But this preference for crunchy foods is part of Jeremy's sensory processing needs. His oral sensory cravings made him seek out textures that were crunchy.

The challenge of feeding a picky eater like Jeremy is one many parents face. Some children might love a particular taste like sour or spicy, while others can't tolerate it at all. In Jeremy's case, he loves sour foods, so I used that to my advantage. I started cooking gravies with a sour taste and adding vegetables he wouldn't normally eat, like bitter gourd. Stir-frying bitter gourd wasn't appealing to him, but once it was cooked in a sour or spicy gravy, it became one of his favorites.

For mothers struggling with picky eaters, it's all about experimenting with different cooking methods. Try different tastes, textures, and combinations to see what your child enjoys. You could serve a small portion of a new vegetable or dish on their plate. Sometimes, when the family is eating something new, and the child sees everyone enjoying it, their curiosity is piqued. They may try a bite just to see what the fuss is about.

In our case, when introducing something new, we would all serve ourselves the new vegetable, talking about how delicious it was without paying attention to Jeremy. It didn't take long before he wanted to try it too. Once he tasted it and liked it, we gently acknowledged it without forcing the issue. The more you push a child to eat, the more resistance you might face. So, keeping it low-pressure can sometimes work best.

It's tough when you keep telling them to eat or try something new because the more you push, the more they won't want to. The best approach is for everyone to sit together at the dining table, with the same food on each plate, and just enjoy the meal. When the child sees everyone else happily eating, they'll eventually become curious.

The rule is that everyone must finish the food on their plate, so at some point, they'll give it a try. Whether they like it or not is something you can figure out from there.

Before making any big changes to your child's diet, it's always a good idea to consult with a healthcare professional or dietitian. They can help guide you on whether the GFCF diet might be right for your child and ensure they still receive proper nutrition while making dietary adjustments.

Chapter 8

Deciding on Medication – When and If It's Needed

Disclaimer

The medication mentioned here is based on the advice of a medical professional specifically for our situation. Every parent or caregiver needs to consult with their own doctor or specialist before considering medication. What works for one child may not work for another, and medication should always be prescribed by a qualified professional who understands the individual needs of your child.

At the point of deciding whether to start Jeremy on medication, was a really tough decision. I didn't have much feedback from other parents about medication. Most of them said their child didn't need it and that their situations were manageable. So, I didn't have many experiences to lean on in this area.

The only advice I got was from the pediatric doctor at the government hospital. The doctor explained, *"Medication is prescribed to children when parents feel they can't cope at all and also when the child cannot be taught or is just too hyper and lacks focus."* The doctor made it clear that the decision to start medication was entirely mine, and that it had to come with my approval.

When I asked about the possible side effects, the doctor mentioned that, in most cases, children tend to gain weight. So, I was advised to control Jeremy's diet and keep him active with exercises to burn off any extra energy.

Based on what the doctor advised, I decided to start Jeremy on medication to see how it would help him. At that time, I had no other choice. I couldn't manage Jeremy, and I didn't have much help. He was just six years old when the hospital started him on a very small dose of 0.01 drops of Risperidone.

It did help. Jeremy became calmer and was able to continue with the training he needed. He also had trouble sleeping, he was always alert and wasn't getting enough rest for a growing child. The medication helped him sleep better, which was a relief. But one issue that came up was his constant hunger. He was always asking for food, and the more active he was, the hungrier he became. Even with regular exercise, he slowly started to gain weight.

During each follow-up visit with the doctor, I was told to control his diet. But the problem with the medication was that once Jeremy's body got used to the dose, it stopped working as well. So, the doctor suggested increasing the dosage to 0.02 drops of Risperidone.

Around that time, I took Jeremy to the Singapore Women's and Children's Hospital, as I mentioned before. The doctors there were surprised that he had started medication so early. In Singapore, they only give medication as a last option, after giving parents proper training and support. Usually, it's not even considered until after the child turns eight, and even then, it's given in the smallest dose possible.

In Singapore, the decision to start medication isn't made by parents alone. It's up to the specialist doctors, and they also provide help to parents, including support from volunteers and organizations to make things easier.

After talking to the doctors in Singapore, I felt sad and disappointed. If I had received better guidance earlier, I might have delayed starting medication for Jeremy. But by that time, it felt too late to change things.

At the next follow-up with the Malaysian doctor, when they wanted to increase the dosage, I chose to keep the lower dose and manage things on my own with other ways to handle the challenges.

Some of Jeremy's classmates were prescribed Ritalin instead of Risperidone. This made the teachers curious about why Jeremy, who was also very hyperactive, wasn't prescribed the same. So, I asked Jeremy's doctor about it.

The doctor explained that Ritalin is typically for kids with ADHD, while Jeremy had both ASD and ADHD. In his case, Risperidone was considered the better option to help him calm down and focus. Jeremy also had other behaviors, like getting easily agitated and showing some signs of aggressiveness. While ADHD's main challenge is hyperactivity, which Ritalin helps manage, Risperidone was chosen because it also addresses some of these additional behaviors.

I noticed that Ritalin worked well for the other children who were taking it. But since Risperidone and Ritalin can't be taken together, Jeremy stuck with Risperidone. While he was on the medication, I made sure to continue with all the necessary therapies and also kept up with his training at home.

Unfortunately, the benefits didn't last. Over time, the medication caused side effects that I hadn't expected. Jeremy started to show mild symptoms of seizures, which led the doctor to stop the medication immediately. Once we stopped, things became even more challenging for both me and the school.

Jeremy's sleeping patterns got worse. He was staying awake late into the night and wasn't eating well either. He had very little appetite and the amount of food he ate decreased. After stopping the medication, Jeremy returned to his very hyperactive self. The school did its best, but it became difficult to get him to sit and focus in class.

I tried to help by increasing his exercise routines, whether at OT sessions or home, to burn off some of his excess energy. I also completely removed sugary foods from his diet, hoping it would help him sleep better. Still, with the added worry about his sleep patterns and the potential for seizures, I decided to take Jeremy to see a neurologist, where we did an EEG to assess his condition.

*An **Electroencephalogram (EEG)** is a medical test used to record brain activity. Small sensors, or electrodes, are placed on the scalp to detect the electrical signals produced by the brain. The test is painless, and the recorded signals are then analyzed by doctors to* *understand various brain functions or identify any irregularities. EEGs are used to diagnose conditions related to the brain, such as* epilepsy, sleep disorders, and brain tumors. *It measures electrical activity, and by studying these signals, doctors can identify if there are any abnormal patterns that indicate underlying neurological issues.*

The challenge with getting the EEG done for Jeremy was making him sleep with all the sensors attached to his head. The recording was done while he was awake and while he was sleeping. The results showed that Jeremy had a condition known as **Epileptic Encephalopathy.**

What shocked us most wasn't just the epilepsy diagnosis but what the EEG showed about how Jeremy's brain worked during sleep. Even though he looked like he was resting, his brain stayed active, meaning he wasn't getting proper rest. This helped explain why his development was slower than expected.

Sleep is very important for children because it helps both their body and brain rest and grow. It's during sleep that the brain processes what they've learned, and their body recharges for the next day. Since Jeremy's brain wasn't fully resting, it was affecting his overall growth and progress.

I also found out that epilepsy is more common in children with autism. We don't know for sure if the medication Jeremy was taking caused the epilepsy, but once he was diagnosed, we had to stop all autism-related medication. After we watched him closely, the doctors put him on medication to stop the seizures from coming back.

The doctors first gave Jeremy Epilim, and later switched to Topiramate, which worked better for him. Thankfully, there haven't been any more incidents of epilepsy. However, after we stopped Risperidone, dealing with Jeremy's behavior and hyperactivity felt like a constant rollercoaster. I found myself always trying to figure out what was causing his mood swings and how to help him manage them.

If you're a parent reading this, I would suggest trying to delay starting medication if possible and exploring all other options first. If your doctor recommends medication, ask about the side effects and check if there are alternative methods you can try before deciding.

Throughout my journey with Jeremy, I've met other parents who faced similar challenges. Some decided not to use medication, even with the difficulties they faced, while others, due to the severity of their child's aggression or hyperactivity, felt they had no choice but to turn to medication. Every child with autism is different, and each situation needs to be looked at individually.

There's no judgment in whether a parent chooses medication or decides to avoid it. If you ask me now, would I have chosen medication for Jeremy if I knew there were other options?

My answer is no, I wouldn't have.

But do I regret starting medication?

Yes, I do regret starting it as early as I did.

Would I have done anything differently at the time?

Honestly, no, because I felt completely lost back then. I didn't know what else to do or where to turn for help, and hiring a behavior therapist wasn't an option in the area I lived in.

During this time, some parents shared alternative methods for calming their children. One example was aromatherapy, a natural way to manage challenging behaviors. They used essential oils, which can help reduce these behaviors. These oils come in various scents and can be inhaled or applied in a diluted form as a massage. Since they're plant-based, they don't have side effects, but it's important to find the right aroma that fits the child's needs.

For Jeremy, I focused on oils that helped with his hyperactivity, behavior, and sleep patterns. It took some time, but I did notice positive changes. If you're interested in trying this, make sure you get good quality oils because there are a lot of fake or less effective ones available. The oils aren't only for behavior-related issues; there are also oils for improving focus, boosting the immune system, reducing anxiety, and promoting relaxation.

Some parents reported big improvements in their children's day-to-day lives, while others didn't see much difference. For Jeremy, the oils helped reduce his anxiety and improved his sleep, though he remained quite hyper, which was always a challenge.

Jeremy was doing well in school and therapy, and we decided to move to a new state to give him more opportunities. It meant starting fresh with new schools and new therapists, but we were lucky to find a good behavioral therapist very soon. Things were going well, until COVID-19 changed everything.

Suddenly, everything stopped. Schools closed, therapy sessions were canceled, and Jeremy had to stay home all day. He didn't understand why he couldn't go outside or why school was canceled. This change made him frustrated, and he started acting out more. He became aggressive and had a lot of tantrums.

With no therapists to help and hospitals focused on COVID patients, we didn't know what to do. Thankfully, with the help of my cousin, I was able to get an online appointment with a doctor. The doctor prescribed some medication to help calm Jeremy down. At that point, I didn't have much of a choice. Jeremy was 14 when he started taking the medication again.

The doctor started with a very small dose of Quetiapine and slowly increased it. Luckily, this time, the medication worked without any side effects. Jeremy was calmer, slept better, and seemed more relaxed.

As things improved with COVID-19, schools reopened, and therapy sessions started again. We took Jeremy out on simple outings, like walks in the park, where it wasn't crowded. Just being outside made him so happy. Staying at home had been really hard for him because he didn't understand why everything had changed.

I know I wasn't the only parent going through this. Some of Jeremy's classmates also struggled during the lockdown, and their parents had to turn to medication to help manage their behaviors.

Now, Jeremy is still on the same medication, and with the help of therapy and school, he's doing much better.

Chapter 9

Exploring Different Treatments and Therapies

When you have a child who needs extra support, you try everything that might help. You read, you talk to other parents, and you explore different options. That's exactly what I did with Jeremy. I wanted to see if there was anything that could make things better for him.

One of the first things I tried was aromatherapy with essential oils as mentioned in chapter 8.

We also tried *Ayurvedic herbal treatment,* a traditional method that uses special oils and herbs. In this treatment, herbs were wrapped around Jeremy's head as part of the process. I committed to doing this continuously for 14 days. Along with this, there was also a body massage included to help improve blood circulation.

I met another mother through Facebook who shared her son's progress through Ayurvedic treatment.

She spent a month at an Ayurvedic center in Kerala, where her son received treatment, followed by supplements to continue at home. According to her, this was a major turning point. This wasn't the first time I had heard about Ayurvedic treatment, so I looked into options available in Malaysia, as traveling to India for treatment wasn't financially possible.

I found that several Ayurvedic centers in Malaysia, run by practitioners from India, offered similar treatments. Since my main challenges with Jeremy were his hyperactivity and sleep issues, the Ayurvedic doctor recommended a herbal treatment for his head. They applied a special herbal paste to his head, wrapped it, and left it on for about 30 minutes.

Initially, Jeremy had trouble sitting still, which made it difficult for the helpers to keep the wrap in place. Thankfully, my brother-in-law and cousin were there to help hold him while the treatment was applied. The first few days were a struggle because Jeremy didn't understand what was happening, but eventually, he became more cooperative once he got used to it.

The treatment lasted 14 days, as prescribed by the Ayurvedic doctor. They also gave some herbal-based supplements to continue after the treatment.

After just three days of treatment, I noticed a big difference in Jeremy. He wasn't running around as much, and he seemed calmer. His teacher even asked if we had started him on a new medication because it was easier to get him to focus in class. As the days passed, he could sit still for longer and seemed happier overall. It felt like a real change.

I couldn't continue with the Ayurvedic treatment because it was hard to get the herbs from India. But I would still tell other parents to give it a try if they are looking for an alternative to regular medication. Of course, every child is different, so the treatment should be based on what your child needs. For Jeremy, the good effects lasted about three months before his old behaviors started to return gradually.

For the best results, it's important to start Ayurvedic treatment as early as possible and stay consistent with it. Make sure you visit a genuine centre and consult a qualified professional in Ayurvedic treatment.

Nutrition soon became an important focus. A child's health depends on proper nutrition, and without it, progress can be slow. Speaking with a nutritionist helped me understand which foods to include in Jeremy's diet and which supplements could support him. This guidance reassured me that he was getting the nutrients he needed to stay healthy.

Alongside improving his diet, I also explored supplements, specifically probiotics and prebiotics, which are known to support gut health. I introduced them gradually, observing how he responded. Over time, I noticed small changes, he seemed more comfortable overall.

As I continued exploring different ways to support Jeremy's well-being, I came across another alternative method that focused on understanding his body's mineral levels. This approach was introduced to me when he was around five years old, through his school principal.

Hair Tissue Mineral Analysis (HTMA) is a method where a small sample of hair is taken and sent to a lab for testing. In Jeremy's case, the sample was sent to Singapore for analysis. The results provided a detailed breakdown of his mineral levels, highlighting any deficiencies or excesses that could affect his overall health. The report also included recommendations on dietary changes and supplements to help restore balance.

I followed this process for Jeremy until he was nine years old, after which I decided to stop, as his diet had become more stable. However, for children with very limited food choices or picky eating habits, this test can be a helpful tool. Doing it once a year can provide insights into the child's nutritional status and guide adjustments in their diet.

While some doctors question how conclusive these tests are, many parents have found them useful in understanding their child's specific needs. Every child is different, and their bodies respond in unique ways as they grow. HTMA can be one way to gain a better understanding of their nutritional health and make informed decisions accordingly.

I looked into therapies that could match his interests and keep him engaged. Every child responds differently to different methods, and I felt it was important to expose him to options beyond the usual routines. That's when I decided to try aqua therapy.

Jeremy has always loved playing in water, so this seemed like a natural choice for him. *Aqua therapy* follows the same principles as occupational therapy but is done in a pool. The water provides a different kind of resistance, helping with strength, coordination, and sensory regulation. Since Jeremy enjoyed being in the water, he responded to it better than OT sessions. His progress in aqua therapy was noticeable, and the experience was positive for him.

The AT coach eventually suggested that I enroll Jeremy in swimming classes. At first, I struggled to find a one-on-one swimming instructor, so I could only send him occasionally. Despite this, the swimming coach gave encouraging feedback, Jeremy picked up swimming techniques well.

As Jeremy grew older, by the time he was around twelve, I realized that OT and AT were no longer relevant. It was difficult to find programs suited for teenagers, and at that stage, I had to look for other ways to keep him active. Swimming turned out to be the best option. It kept him physically fit, and more importantly, it was something he loved.

One of the biggest challenges for any parent is letting go, allowing their child to do things independently. There is always a fear of them getting hurt, being mistreated, or facing difficulties on their own. Of course, safety is important, and as parents, we always need to make sure they are in the right place and surrounded by the right people. But at the same time, learning through experience is just as important.

I've seen parents who don't want to take their eyes off their child even for a second, afraid that something might go wrong. While this is understandable, it can also make the child overly dependent. They may struggle to do things on their own because they have always relied on someone else. Finding a balance is important, ensuring their safety while also giving them the space to grow and learn from their own experiences.

Kids have different strengths and challenges to catch up with their growth.

If your child enjoys sports or any physical activities, trying out a sports and recreational park could be a good option. In Malaysia, most of these parks are indoors and offer age-appropriate activities. There are different kinds of setups, and you can explore based on what your child is comfortable with. Some have trampoline jumps, rock climbing, or free-fall activities, making it an exciting experience. Many parents have shared how much their children with ASD and ADHD enjoy these classes. It's like a full-body workout, which can have a positive impact on both their energy levels and focus.

At the same time, some children prefer creative activities. If a child enjoys art, simply providing them with the right tools and materials can bring out great results. I remember learning about a young girl named Jamila from Malaysia, who has autism. Despite her challenges, she does very well in her own way. Her parents discovered that she thrived when given the right activities to focus on. Art brought her joy and calmness, so they supported her by giving her the space and tools to create. Over time, it became more than just a hobby, it became a way for her to express herself and build confidence.

Stories like hers show how important it is to recognize what makes a child feel comfortable and engaged.

The same goes for music. If a child shows interest in playing an instrument or learning music, attending specialized classes could help nurture their talent. Children who are naturally drawn to music tend to pick it up quickly, and with the right guidance, they can do well in it.

Yoga is something some parents have tried, and it has helped their children in different ways. It improves balance, coordination, and flexibility, which can be useful for daily activities. The slow movements and stretches can also help children feel more relaxed. Some parents have noticed that their children seem calmer after a yoga session.

For children who can sit and follow simple instructions, yoga can be a good way to improve focus and body control. The movements are gentle, and they can go at their own pace. It is not about doing every pose perfectly but about getting used to moving their bodies in a steady and controlled way. Some children enjoy it, and for those who do, it can be a fun and useful activity to add to their routine. This one did not work for Jeremy.

But as children grow, parents start thinking beyond daily activities. The bigger concern is preparing them for independence. Every parent of a child with special needs wonders about the future, how their child will manage on their own and what options are available to help them develop the right skills.

For a long time, I looked into different possibilities, including boarding schools for children with special needs. I wanted to understand how these schools worked and whether they could be an option for Jeremy in the future. Some schools in countries like India, Indonesia, and the Philippines focused on helping children become more independent. While I wasn't considering sending Jeremy overseas, I wanted to learn about these schools to see if something similar existed in Malaysia.

Another option I came across was the *fostering home concept.* In this setup, a child lives with a family that has experience handling children with special needs. They are trained in a structured home environment to develop independence. Some parents I spoke to said their children adjusted well and learned life skills much faster in these settings. But for non-verbal children like Jeremy, there was always a risk. If something went wrong or if they were mistreated, they wouldn't be able to express it. That concern stayed with me.

Some children enjoy these environments because they are surrounded by others like them, friends who understand them, a space where they feel accepted without judgment. That kind of setting can make a big difference in their confidence and growth.

For Jeremy, I knew that a boarding school or fostering home wasn't the right choice when he was younger. His biggest challenge had always been behavior, and I was advised to explore other ways to help him before considering a major transition like that. But I kept researching because I knew that as he grew older, I might have to revisit the idea.

One of my biggest concerns was that Jeremy was growing taller and stronger than me. As a mother, I worried that there would come a time when I wouldn't be able to manage him physically. I needed to plan ahead and find ways to help him develop skills to live with less dependence on me. At home, he relied on me for many things, and I wanted to see if he could function in an environment without family constantly around him.

Jeremy's long-time behavioral therapist and child psychologist, Miss Megan Woods, has been supporting him for years. Her sessions aim to help him unlearn negative behaviors and habits and adopt better ones. Although the training center was effective, things were different at home. He would follow rules when the therapist was present, but sometimes he refused to do so with me. This wasn't misbehavior; he simply saw me as his mother rather than a teacher. Like many teenagers, he tested boundaries.

Then I came across the story of a Singaporean mother with a non-verbal son with autism. Her son was growing older, and she was beginning to feel worried about how she would continue caring for him as he became bigger and stronger. She found a boarding school in Bali specifically designed for children with autism who needed extra help learning to live more independently. At first, she was unsure. The thought of her son, who couldn't speak to express his feelings, living away from her was difficult. She wondered if he would feel abandoned, or if he would understand why she made this choice.

The school in Bali was set up to support children with autism in all areas of daily life. It provided a stable, structured environment with familiar routines and staff trained to help children develop essential skills. They worked on everything from self-care, like dressing and eating, to building social connections. Over time, her son adjusted to the new environment, growing more comfortable with each day. The school reported back to her that he was engaging with activities, interacting with other children, and learning to handle daily tasks with confidence. He even formed bonds with other students, and she felt reassured knowing he was finding a sense of belonging.

Hearing this story made me see boarding school in a new way. I realised that giving Jeremy this chance wasn't about stepping back; it was about giving him a chance to grow and learn. I thought, *"If it works out, that's wonderful. If it doesn't, I can always bring him back."* I felt I could try it and see if it could offer him the skills and experiences he needed to grow.

As he got older, Miss Megan started a vocational training center called Thoughtful Minds in Malaysia. The center was designed to help children with special needs learn practical skills that would help them become more independent. I had known Miss Megan for years, and she had been a big part of Jeremy's progress. If there was anyone I could trust to guide him, it was her.

He attended training there regularly, but I knew I needed to take another step. That's when I decided to try the boarding program at Thoughtful Minds.

And, my siblings encouraged me to give it a try, I finally took the step I had been afraid of for so long.

At first, I was nervous because, Jeremy had never stayed away from us before. I sent him for a trial period, bringing him home on weekends to see how he adjusted. I followed up with the school daily to check how he was doing. The teachers shared that while he was initially confused, probably wondering why I hadn't come to pick him up like I usually did, he adapted well. He connected with the other children, and the teachers had positive feedback.

By the second week, I told him in the car, *"Mama is sending you back to boarding school, and I'll pick you up for the weekend, okay?"* He just smiled. That was reassuring. As we drove, he recognized the route and started smiling and laughing. That's when I knew he was happy there. The moment we arrived, he got out of the car, walked in, and closed the door himself.

Sending Jeremy to boarding school turned out to be one of the best decisions I made. In just a month, I saw changes in him. His behavior improved, and the teachers at Thoughtful Minds even visited our home to guide me on how to maintain his routines. Their advice was practical, and it made a real difference.

The financial support from my sister, brother, and cousin made all of this possible, and I will always be grateful to them. While I was only able to send Jeremy to full-time boarding for two months, I still make sure he goes once a week for continued training. During school holidays, he spends a full week there, and he enjoys it.

There are many different approaches that parents explore to support their children's development. Each method has its own purpose, and while some may show progress, others may not have the same effect. Among the many options, one more method that has been discussed is stem cell therapy.

I first heard about *stem cell therapy* when I attended a talk by a doctor who explained how it could help children with special needs. The doctor mentioned that the earlier the treatment is started, the better the chances of seeing progress, as a young child's brain is still developing. Since Jeremy was already ten years old by the time I learned about it, I decided not to proceed. However, I still wanted to understand more about how it worked.

Stem cell therapy is based on the idea of repairing specific areas of the brain, particularly neurons that may not be functioning properly. Stem cells are known for their ability to support these neurons, helping them work more effectively.

For those who want to learn more about MSC therapy, it is always best to speak to a doctor or professional who can provide accurate information. Research on this treatment is ongoing, and while it may be helpful for some, it is important to gather as much information as possible before making any decisions.

Mesenchymal Stem Cells (MSCs) are found in various parts of the body, such as bone marrow, fat tissue, and umbilical cord tissue. These cells have a unique ability to transform into different types of cells, including bone, cartilage, and muscle cells. Because of this, they have been studied for their role in healing and repairing damaged tissues.

One of the most important functions of MSCs is their ability to help with tissue repair. When the body experiences injury or inflammation, these cells move to the affected area and support the healing process by releasing substances that reduce inflammation and promote tissue recovery.

For children with autism, researchers are studying how MSCs might help by reducing brain inflammation and improving the connections between brain cells. This could potentially lead to improvements in social skills, communication, and behavior. While early research shows promise, MSC therapy for autism is still being studied. More research is needed to confirm its effectiveness and the best way to use it.

I also heard from a mother whose son, Ethan, went through mesenchymal stem cell (MSC) therapy. She noticed positive changes after the treatment. His response time improved, his eye contact became better, and he seemed more aware of his surroundings. His senses became sharper, and even his immune system appeared stronger. These were the noticeable improvements she shared with me.

There are many treatments and therapies being explored to support children with autism. Some focus on nutrition, others on physical activity, while some look at medical approaches like stem cell therapy. Research continues, and every parent has to make informed choices based on what they feel is right for their child.

Disclaimer

The information provided in this section is based on personal experiences and general research. Stem cell therapy, including Mesenchymal Stem Cell (MSC) therapy, is still being studied, and its effectiveness for autism has not been fully established. Every child is different, and what works for one may not work for another.

If you are considering this treatment, it is important to consult with a qualified medical professional. They can provide accurate, up-to-date information and guide you on whether this approach may be suitable for your child. Always gather as much information as possible and make decisions based on professional advice and thorough research.

While there is no single answer, learning about different methods can help in understanding what options are available.

Chapter 10

Taking Care of Yourself as a Parent

Being a parent to a child with ASD, ADHD, or any special needs can feel overwhelming. You can easily lose yourself while trying to manage all the responsibilities. If you're wondering how I handled everything, the truth is, I didn't do it perfectly.

That's why I decided to write this book, to share my experiences, the good and the difficult moments. As parents, we often try to do everything, but it's important to realize that it's okay to let some things go. For me, I had to stop trying to keep the house spotless and follow a perfect routine. At some point, I even stopped taking time for myself because I thought all my focus should be on my son.

But when I stopped taking care of myself, things got harder. I felt more stressed and disconnected from everyone. Whenever I thought about doing something for myself, I felt guilty, like I wasn't doing enough as a mother.

I learned that taking care of yourself is not wrong. It's necessary.

Looking after yourself is like a lifeguard trying to save someone. The lifeguard needs a life jacket first to be able to help. Without it, both could end up in trouble. The same thing happens to us as parents. When we feel overwhelmed, our moods and emotions change, and your child will sense that.

There's no such thing as a perfect mother. That idea is a myth. Even those who seem perfect have their own struggles, though we may not see them. Parents, especially those caring for a child with special needs, face a lot of pressure. On top of the stress, we also need to be understanding of our family members, who are feeling their own stress.

If you're a working mom, it's even harder to balance everything, work, family, and caring for your child. It's a lot to handle, and we are only human. Some days will be tough, and others will be better. And that's okay. You are not alone in this. Many parents, including myself, have gone through the same ups and downs.

Some parents, including me, have had meltdowns. I always thought I was strong enough to handle anything. The weight of everything became too much and pushed me towards anxiety. I couldn't sleep, I couldn't eat, and sometimes I would tremble. At that point, I wasn't thinking clearly, and I started to forget things.

My heart would race, and I felt like my emotions were on a rollercoaster. I didn't know what was happening to me, so I went to the doctor. The doctor immediately told me that these were symptoms of anxiety, and they needed to be addressed quickly. The doctor gave me some medication, but it made me feel worse.

With a referral letter, I went to see a psychiatrist. That visit was a real wake-up call for me. The psychiatrist asked me about my life and wanted to know what I was doing every day. I talked about my routine, and then the doctor started asking questions.

"What do you do for yourself outside of your daily tasks?" I couldn't answer. I was completely blank. Slowly, I said, *"Nothing. My time is fully taken up with what I need to do for my son and family."*

Then came more questions: *"What are your hobbies? What do you enjoy? When was the last time you went out with friends?"*

I didn't have answers for any of them. I had no hobbies. I hadn't done anything just for myself in a long time.

At the end of the session, the doctor told me I needed to take up something I enjoyed again. He suggested I think back to what I loved doing before I became a mother and start there. It didn't have to be something big. The doctor told me to take up a hobby like yoga, gardening, or art to help calm my mind. Even something small like that would be helpful. The doctor prescribed medication, but I decided not to take it. I realized where I had gone wrong, **I needed a break.**

That's when, as I mentioned earlier, I went on a yoga retreat with complete strangers. It brought me a lot of clarity about myself and my thinking.

Journaling about how I ended up in this situation helped me a lot. It gave me a chance to reflect, slow down, and make changes in my routine. Whenever I had the opportunity, I started doing things outside my usual schedule. These early stages were full of challenges, but looking back, I can now see how much I've grown. As you go through this journey with your special child, you will also realize how much you've learned and how strong you've become.

It's important to appreciate yourself and celebrate the small victories. It doesn't have to be something big. I once read about a practice where you take a jar and small pieces of paper. Each time your child accomplishes something, no matter how small, write it down and put it in the jar. You can even do the same for yourself. At the end of the month or year, open the jar and read what you wrote. It gives you a sense of accomplishment, reminding you of all the progress, even in the smallest moments.

Looking back, I now understand why many of us feel emotionally overwhelmed. There's always so much expected of us to help our child make progress. On top of that, we often ignore our own bodies when they tell us to take a break.

Self-care really is important. It helps you recharge, physically, emotionally, and mentally. You'll notice that after taking a break, your mind is clearer, and you feel more energized.

Another thing that affected me was how people would constantly ask about Jeremy's progress. Friends and family, like cousins, would often ask me why I hadn't tried certain treatments or therapies. In the beginning, I found myself repeating the same answers over and over again. After a while, it became draining. Each time I had to explain, it felt like I was losing a part of myself. It was mentally exhausting.

Not everyone who asks, *"Is your child okay?"* or *"Has there been any improvement?"* is really there to help. Often, people are just curious. They want to know what's going on, and after you share, the conversation usually ends. That's where it stops.

But with advice from people who really care, I learned to approach these questions differently. When someone asks how Jeremy is doing, I simply say, "He's okay, he's making progress." If they ask if he's talking, I tell them, "One word at a time." If they suggest trying something I've already heard of, I say, "Yes, I'm aware of it, and I'm already doing it."

If they suggest something new, I ask for more details. If they genuinely want to help, they'll have more to share or will follow up later. If not, that might be the last time we talk about it, and that's fine. I can always look up more information myself and decide if it's worth trying.

Learning new things is always good, and sometimes a suggestion might be helpful. By answering kindly and positively, I found that people started asking fewer questions. If you want peace of mind, the best way to handle these situations is to stay polite and positive. People aren't always trying to be hurtful; they're just curious. But for us, as parents dealing with many challenges, answering too many questions can feel tiring.

It takes time for others to accept things, just as it took time for me when I first learned about Jeremy's diagnosis. We can't expect everyone around us to understand right away. But that doesn't mean you should keep everything to yourself. You know who really cares and will listen without judgment. Talking to those people can help lighten the load you're carrying.

Sometimes, you may wonder why people don't understand your situation. It's often because they've never been through it themselves. Some might know about ASD or ADHD but aren't really interested in learning more. They just want to check in on your child's progress. That's okay. You can answer kindly and move on.

The best support often comes from other parents in similar situations. Talking to them can give you new ideas and make you feel less alone.

Another thing that helps is sharing responsibilities with your family. Don't feel like you need to do everything yourself. If you try to handle everything on your own, you might burn out. Some parents even give small tasks to their children, which can be a helpful practice.

I must admit, I started giving tasks to Jeremy a bit later than I should have. What may seem like a simple task to one family could be different for another. The key is to assign tasks that are appropriate for your child. For example, things like tidying up toys after playing, watering the plants, putting dirty clothes in the washing machine, or washing dishes after a meal. Even clearing the dinner table can be helpful.

Children won't do these tasks perfectly, but if they can follow a routine, it's already a big help for parents. It's not just about them learning responsibility; it also makes the load lighter for you.

Another thing to consider is looking back at your hobbies or interests, something you loved doing but stopped. That could be a good reason to start taking time for yourself again.

Fathers, too, need breaks. While they provide financial support, they also tend to overlook their own self-care. Men often keep their emotions quiet, not wanting to add stress to the challenges mothers face. But fathers need time for themselves as well. Both parents do. It's important for both the mother and father to take a break from the routine, to have those moments of "me time."

But also, don't forget about spending time together. The child is a shared responsibility, but the marriage is, too. When I spoke to other parents, many said that the things they used to enjoy as a couple slowly faded away. In some cases, those activities stopped entirely, with one partner focusing on providing financial support while the other took care of the child.

This can lead to couples losing sight of each other. Sometimes, marriages struggle, especially when one partner feels overwhelmed. Some couples stay together to support the child, but the connection they had before the child was born starts to fade. If you feel like this, know that it's not unusual.

This is common, especially among middle-class families where the cost of raising a special child can feel overwhelming. But it's important to make time for each other. Even if it's just a quiet dinner without talking about the child, it can do wonders for your relationship.

Mrs. Chan, as I mentioned earlier, did this well. With the help of a maid to care for her son, she found time for herself and her husband. They made it a point to connect, which helped them stay strong as a couple. At this point, I noticed that there are many healthy practices and tips available online that support self-care for parents with ADHD and ASD children. You can also join support groups if available. This group helps people connect and share their journeys, which can make you feel less alone. These small steps can make a big difference in helping parents maintain balance.

Have You Heard of "Laughter is the Best Medicine"?

Well, it's true. Laughter increases the brain's production of endorphins, which helps reduce stress and pain. I came across an article about reducing stress, and I tried out one of the suggestions. If you are at a comedy show and laughing at the jokes, that's great. But even if you're not, you can still fake it and feel the benefits.

You start with a *"ha,"* then a *"ha ha,"* and then *"ha ha ha ha."* By the time you get to the fifth "ha," I found myself genuinely laughing. Some people might even start laughing before that. It's amazing how light you feel emotionally when you laugh. You can try it out, it's a simple way to relieve stress.

Another thing I've found helpful when things feel overwhelming is to simply stop. Sometimes, when everything is too much, I take a break. One of my favorite ways to unwind is by listening to music. There's one song by Bruno Mars called "The Lazy Song." The lyrics say, "Today I don't feel like doing anything." It's followed by a list of all the things the singer doesn't want to do. I add my own lyrics like, "I don't want to clean up. I don't want to cook. I don't want to drive." Just like the song says, I don't want to do anything.

Listening to that song, or any music I love, helps me a lot when stress builds up. Music has a way of calming the mind. When nothing else works, I pick up the phone and call my siblings. I'm blessed to have a sister and a brother who are my biggest support. Just talking to them helps me feel lighter.

Sometimes, just having a conversation with someone you trust, like a sibling or a best friend, can make a big difference. If you're feeling overwhelmed, don't hesitate to make that call. It helps more than you might think.

Conclusion

In these 18 years with Jeremy, what I want to say is **Never Give Up**. Do the best you can. Don't expect everything to go perfectly, and take each day as it comes. Remember to take care of yourself too. Whatever faith you believe in, pray for guidance for you and your child.

Once, a nun told me something that stayed with me. She said, *"Your child is special in the eyes of God, and you are the chosen one to care for this blessed child."* At that time, I felt lost and unsure of what to do. But when I look back, I see that every time I faced a challenge and didn't know where to turn, help came. Sometimes it was family, other times friends, or even someone I barely knew. It felt like I was never left alone to figure it out, and I believe that was God's way of guiding me.

If you find that your child is good at something, help them grow in that area. But if you don't see anything special yet, that is fine too. The most important thing is to help them become as independent as possible. Teach them how to care for themselves, from waking up in the morning to getting ready for bed at night. Take small steps and build from there.

Every stage of life brings new challenges. Treat each challenge as a chance to learn. If something doesn't work, try something else. Mistakes happen, and that is alright. What matters is that you keep moving forward.

If I could go back in time, there are things I would do differently. But I have no regrets. Every mistake taught me something valuable. Some of those mistakes turned into the best lessons I learned. For that, I am grateful.

Remember, we can't figure everything out all at once. Take it one step at a time. With support from family, professionals, and the people around you, you'll feel more ready to face the challenges that come your way. When I feel low or unsure, I listen to motivational talks to help me think positively. These talks remind me to keep going, even on hard days.

I've also learned so much from conversations with other parents of special needs children. Their stories and experiences gave me strength and helped me believe in myself. I'm deeply grateful for every parent I've met along this journey.

One of my favorite motivational speakers is Robin Sharma. Two quotes from him stay with me always. The first is, *"Make your faith larger than your fears and your dreams bigger than your doubts."* The second is, *"Change is hard at first, messy in the middle, and gorgeous at the end."* These words remind me that even though the road is tough at times, trusting in God and in yourself will help you move forward. Over time, when you look back at how far you've come, you'll see that you've done well.

Celebrate your efforts and your child's progress. Don't compare your journey with anyone else's. Your journey with your child is unique and special in its own way.

If you can, share your experiences with parents who are just beginning this path. Your story could give them the courage to face their own challenges. Sharing truly is caring.

My prayer for you, dear reader, is that my journey has inspired you and offered some guidance to help you move forward.

May your faith light your way and guide you on the right path.

About the Author

Angeline Shanta spent the first five years of her career working as an administrator before transitioning to the Human Resources Department. During this time, she completed her MBA at the University of Southern Queensland, specializing in Human Resources. Her expertise lies in hiring, payroll management, and training.

Shanta's passion for connecting with people made her role in the training department especially fulfilling, as she enjoyed mentoring and grooming newly hired employees. After dedicating 25 years to her professional career, she decided to take a break to focus on her family.

Her life took a new direction when she was blessed with a son, leading her on a journey of learning, growth, and self-discovery. This experience inspired her to share her story, offering insights and support to parents and families facing similar challenges.

www.ingramcontent.com/pod-product-compliance
Lightning Source LLC
Chambersburg PA
CBHW020611160726
47991CB00002BA/723